Myths of Mindfulness

Myths of Mindfulness

by Richard W. Sears

First published in 2021 by Sequoia Books

ISBN
Print: 9781914110061
EPUB: 9781914110078

A CIP record for this book is available from the British Library

Library of Congress Cataloguing-In-Publication Data
Name: Richard W. Sears, author
Title: Talent to Triumph: How Athletes Turn Potential Into High Performance / Richard W. Sears
Description: 1st Edition, Sequoia Books UK 2021
Print: 9781914110061
EPUB: 9781914110078

Library of Congress Control Number: 2021916770

Print and Electronic production managed by Deanta Global

Cover designed by Kelly Miller

Dedication

To my wife, Carrie, for helping me see through the myths of relationships.

About the Author

Richard W. Sears, PsyD, PhD, MBA, ABPP is a board-certified clinical psychologist, mindfulness instructor, and Zen teacher living in southwest Ohio, USA. He runs a private psychology and consultation practice, conducts workshops on mindfulness and other topics online and around the world, and is Director of the Center for Clinical Mindfulness & Meditation. He is also an annual adjunct professor of psychology at the University of Cincinnati, clinical/research faculty at the UC Center for Integrative Health and Wellness, and a volunteer professor of clinical psychiatry & behavioral neurosciences with the UC College of Medicine. He has been on a number of research teams investigating the effects of mindfulness on stress, mental health disorders, and how mindfulness changes the brain.

Dr. Sears is author of over a dozen books, including *Mindfulness: Living Through Challenges and Enriching Your Life in This Moment*, *The CBT & Mindfulness Toolbox*, *The Sense of Self*, and *ACT with Anxiety*. He is a licensed private pilot and a light sport airplane mechanic, has a fifth-degree black belt in To-Shin Do/Ninjutsu, and once served as a personal protection agent for the Dalai Lama of Tibet. He has a PhD in Buddhist studies, and received ordination in three traditions, as well as recognition as a Zen master from Wonji Dharma in the lineage of Seung Sahn. You can join an online group or listen to free recordings on Dr. Sears's website, www.psych-insights.com/mindfulness.

Contents

CONTENTS

Acknowledgments

First and foremost, I would like to thank Andrew Peart of Sequoia Books for approaching me to write this book and for supporting me throughout this process.

This book is the culmination of decades of practicing and teaching mindfulness. I would like to thank the many students and mentors who shared with me their ideas, passions, and questions, challenging me to continuously refine my own embodiment of the practice.

As with everything in life, the content of this book is the product of a great many influences. I have been trained and inspired by so many others that it is quite possible (and in fact highly likely) that I used many of their ideas without acknowledging them, but I will do my best to give credit where it is due.

I am very appreciative of the support and inspiration of countless professional colleagues, friends, and mentors on the path of self-exploration, including the Dalai Lama, Wonji Dharma, Suhita Dharma, Steven C. Hayes, Stephen K. Hayes, Zindel Segal, Jon Kabat-Zinn, Elana Rosenbaum, Lane Pederson, Dennis Tirch, D.J. Moran, Robyn Walser, Marsha Linehan, Susan Woods, Randye Semple, Jean Kristeller, Ryan Niemiec, Susan Albers, Sarah Bowen, Ruth Baer, Mark Lau, Alan Marlatt, Dan Siegel, Alan Watts, Sian Cotton, Melissa DelBello, Jeffery Strawn, Rachel Wasson, Kathleen Chard, Tina Luberto, Kristen Kraemer, Emily O'Bryan, Steve and Sandi Amoils, Robert

Brian Denton, Sharon Salzberg, David Kyutoshi Sink, Karuna Bodhi Grafton, and John Ryongwan Paulson, to name but a few.

I would also like to thank the wonderful people on the Acceptance and Commitment Therapy listserv who offered their support and ideas: Sandro Voi, Neil Levitsky, John Powell, Jesse Moreno, Ethan Lester, Peter Hitchcock, Amy Murrell, Cameron Murphey, Lindsay-Jo Sevier-Guy, and Thomas Szabo.

And of course, I am very thankful for the love and support of my family, and for their patience with my countless days of isolation to write and to travel to give workshops: Carrie Mason-Sears, Caylee Sears, Ashlyn and Lizon Karim; Brittney, Olivia, and Violet Taylor; and Linda and John Coghill.

Introduction

Mindfulness, mindfulness, mindfulness. This term has been booming in popularity in recent years in many areas, such as mental health interventions and corporate settings. Mindfulness has also become increasingly popular in mainstream culture, featured on the cover of publications such as *Time* magazine and *The New York Times*.

Recently, on the television program *60 Minutes*, Anderson Cooper basically said at first that it sounded to him like people who practiced mindfulness seemed a bit cult-like. However, he decided to go on a retreat with mindfulness teacher Jon Kabat-Zinn to experience it for himself. Later in the program, Anderson Cooper was hooked up to an EEG monitor, and he was able to change his own brain waves at will. By the end of the program, he said, "I drank the Kool-Aid!" While that is not a very good expression, since drinking the Kool-Aid means you are killing yourself based on false beliefs, I took that to mean that he now practices mindfulness, which is very useful when you interview people for a living.

I began practicing mindfulness as a teenager and have been both excited and concerned about the "mindfulness boom." While there are literally thousands of scientific research studies on mindfulness, there is a tendency to oversell its benefits, which can sometimes even lead to public harm (Rosenbaum & Magid, 2016; Van Dam, van Vugt, Vago, Schmalzl, Saron, et al., 2018).

This tendency to popularize and enthusiastically promote mindfulness without a deeper understanding of the practice and of the scientific study of its uses and limitations has been dubbed "McMind-fulness" (Hyland, 2015; Purser, 2019; Purser & Loy, 2013). Whenever something becomes popularized, misinformation is spread due to the necessity to quickly simplify the transmission of that information. This is all the more true in recent years with the ability of social media to quickly spread that information and misinformation.

The purpose of this book is to explore a number of popular myths that have developed about mindfulness. Myth does not necessarily mean falsehood. It is a way of making sense of things (Watts, 1958, 2004a). Some of the myths we will explore have a factual foundation. Even ones that are completely wrong may have some basis in truth. Most, however, even though they may contain some truth, are not completely accurate.

Some readers may feel it is wrong to tear apart myths about some-thing that gives them hope and comfort. But false hope is of little comfort in the long run. In my experience, facing the realities, and exploring the larger implications of what mindfulness really is and can do, provides far more hope and comfort than do the myths. When you let go of false ideas, reality can be so much richer and more fulfilling.

My own journey in the formal practice of mindfulness began over 35 years ago. It was an integral part of the Zen, Buddhist, and Nin-jutsu martial arts training I began as a teenager. At first, it seemed to me that mindfulness was a special thing that other people had that I did not have, so I imitated others. Once I experienced some of the benefits of mindfulness, I began trying to convince others of what I had been told. Eventually, I began to embody it in my own life, and no longer needed to convince or be convinced of anything. I have found this same pattern play out in Zen, martial arts, and clinical psychology.

In my 30s, I became a clinical psychologist and felt blessed to be a part of the wave of research to incorporate mindfulness into clinical practice. It has been fascinating to watch and participate in the move-ment to improve mental health and well-being through empirically validated mindfulness-based treatments. Most of my career has been centered on teaching mindfulness to the public and to other clinicians, and on clarifying the myths and misconceptions surrounding it.

What I share in this book comes from my lived experiences as well as my understanding of the research I have read and done myself. While I have endeavored to support my assertions in this book with scientific studies, I have been unable to resist drawing on my four decades of experience in practicing mindfulness. However, even in presenting information from a practitioner's and Zen master's point of view, I have tried to make my points in easily understood common sense terms that do not require any mysterious information or leaps of faith.

Defining Mindfulness

Before we investigate the popular myths of mindfulness throughout this book, it may be helpful to explore a working definition. Keep in mind not to take any definition too seriously, as we are using words to describe mindfulness, which is a sensory process that is indescribable in words.

My favorite definition of mindfulness comes from one of its pioneers in adapting it to a modern audience, Jon Kabat-Zinn: Mindfulness is the awareness that emerges, through paying attention, in a particular way: on purpose, in the present moment, and nonjudgmentally, to the unfolding of experience from moment to moment (Kabat-Zinn, 2003, 2013).

We will be talking about all of the aspects of this definition throughout this book, but in summary, mindfulness simply refers to the process of paying attention. You have to be awake to pay attention. You can only pay attention on purpose and in the present moment. You cannot pay attention to the present moment when your mind is compulsively lost in making comparisons to other times and places. And of course, you can pay attention as life unfolds.

Paying attention counters the tendency to live in one's head on automatic pilot. Many of my clients tell me, "It feels like my life is simply waking up, feeding the kids, going to work, coming home to feed the kids, and going to bed. How did I get so old?" Time seems to fly by when we live in our heads, busy thinking of the next things we have to do, and sadly, thinking about regrets we have about past times we did not fully experience because we were busy thinking about the future.

In psychotherapy, I help clients develop awareness of automatic pilot modes of thinking, automatic pilot modes of emotionally reacting, and automatic pilot modes of behavior. These patterns may be useful in some situations, or might have served them in the past, but they can cause problems if they do them automatically without paying attention to the present context.

Being versus Doing

Though it may be a somewhat arbitrary distinction, mindfulness is often described as a way of "being," which is more present focused, in contrast to the mode many of us get stuck in, which is "doing" or future focused.

We are all born with the capacity to simply "be," and all young children are naturally curious. All of the children in the picture below are riveted on the butterfly that the teacher is showing to the class. To a child, a butterfly is a magical being. It has beautiful, fragile wings, and it can float through the air. However, when we grow older, we tend to ignore butterflies, and we might even see them as a nuisance if they fly into the house.

Children have a natural ability to be fully present in the moment. When my daughter was three, I once told her that I would take her to the local ice cream shop after school one day soon. The next day, she jumped into the car and said excitedly, "Hi Daddy! Are we getting ice cream today?" I had to tell her, "Sorry Honey, but I told your mommy that we would meet her at the store right now. We'll get ice cream tomorrow." You should have seen the look on her little face. "Tomorrow?!?! But, I've waited my whole life for ice cream!!!" To her young mind, 24 hours was a lot of now moments, and perhaps even a significant percentage of her life. However, as we grow older, we tend to become much more future focused.

Alan Watts (2004a) talks about the trick that is played on us as we are growing up. The trick is that the good things in life, the "golden goodies," are all coming in the future. There is also an implied caveat that the good things will come faster if you postpone present moment pleasures and work really hard. When you are old enough you get to go to grade school, where you will learn all kinds of cool stuff to prepare you for middle school. In middle school, you learn stuff to prepare you for high school. You better do well in high school, so you can get into college, then maybe graduate school, so you can live the glamorous lifestyle of a professional. And then you can get a good job, so you can get money. And once you get money, you can buy great stuff, like a house. And you better work some extra hours so you can pay off that house. And you better take that promotion so you can save for retirement, when you can get back to just sitting still and enjoying the moment again (if you can live that long with your health intact).

Most of us wake up one day, somewhere around middle age, and realize, "Hey! Wait a minute! I've been tricked! THIS is my life! It's not coming, it's not out there somewhere, it's not someday. I'm in my life right now!" And we feel a little cheated, because we spent most of our lives waiting for life to start, instead of enjoying life as it was happening.

Of course, it is very important to take time to learn from the past, and it can be enjoyable to reminisce about younger days. It is also very important to plan for the future, to have direction and goals for your life. However, if you are always living in those other times in your mind, you will miss out on the present moment, and past lessons and future goals will not be able to come to fruition in your daily life.

Some people have a really hard time with just being. If they sit still too long, they get antsy. But if you cannot be comfortable in the present moment, where will running around in your mind or your life really get you? This anxious feeling is often due to the activation of the stress response system, which was only meant to operate short term, and creates all kinds of health problems when it is firing long term. When you practice sitting still, or just being present in whatever activity you are doing, the antsy feelings will begin to calm down, and the richness of this moment will become much more apparent.

Structure of This Book

Each of the myths that we will explore in this book will be broken down into several sections. First, the popular *myth* itself will be described, along with common variations. Next, we will explore the *basis in truth* for the myth, and any underlying reasons why the myth came to be. Then, the actual *reality* will be compared and contrasted with what is purported by the myth. Although I will endeavor to support my writing with scientific references whenever possible, I hope the reader will also allow me to indulge in making common sense arguments and in playful storytelling to make my points. Next, I will provide a *summary* of the main points. Finally, I will list *further resources* to help you independently get started with your own research to learn more about that particular topic.

Interestingly, though people tend to perpetuate the misconceptions about mindfulness they hear, when they practice it for themselves, they tend to rate similarly on mindfulness measures to those who do have an accurate conceptualization (Lester & Murrell, 2019). Similarly, even ancient Zen masters like Dahui (Broughton & Watanabe, 2017) repeatedly stated that an intellectual understanding will only be misleading, and that one can only wake up through direct experience. In this book, I will attempt to clarify myths and misconceptions about mindfulness, but the absolute best way to do this is to practice it for yourself. After all, words pale in comparison with full sensory experiences. There are many training resources available today, but you are welcome to begin with free recordings of mindfulness practices on my own website, www.psych-insights.com.

1 Myths about the Origins of Mindfulness

We will begin by exploring myths about where mindfulness comes from. Mindfulness has exploded in popularity in recent years, but it is far from new. So where and when did it develop?

If we define mindfulness as simply paying attention in the present moment, then it has been around since the ancestors of our human species. Those who could be keenly aware of their surroundings had a distinct advantage. Those who could feel and avoid painful experiences, who could smell food, who could hear predators approaching, who could detect the taste of poisonous plants, and who could see potential mates clearly were more likely to survive.

As the human brain evolved, it developed the ability to remember events of the past verbally and visually, so that it could learn and adapt from those experiences. It also developed the ability to plan for the future, to take steps to be prepared for potential danger and to secure food and shelter in case of famine or bad weather. The ability to create and work with mental representations facilitated problem-solving skills. All of this had great survival value, and hence allowed our species to survive and thrive.

Of course, the ability to create mental representations, to ruminate about the past, and to worry about the future came with a cost. The human mind linked the stress response to mental representations as well as to physical reality. Instead of only feeling stress when seeing a lion, the stress response would fire when remembering or imagining a lion. As human beings gathered into family groups, tribes, and communities, it became more and more necessary to remember, plan, and problem-solve. The stress response became more frequent and common as a motivator to be prepared for living.

Hence, making time to do things like sitting still and enjoying a sunset became a spiritual experience, in the sense of feeling connected to the environment and other living creatures. Setting aside the active problem-solving mind reminded people of bigger picture values. Instead of only worrying and striving to go on living and striving, remembering to pay attention kept people in touch with what made life precious and meaningful. Perhaps for this reason, all of the major world religions have adopted some form of mindfulness or other contemplative practice.

Let's explore now the basis in truth and the reality of several myths about the origins of mindfulness.

Myth: Mindfulness is strictly a religious practice. Many people are not interested in mindfulness because they associate it with religion. In fact, in one study, over half of those surveyed said they believe mindfulness is a strictly religious practice (Lester, Murrell, & Dickson, 2018).

Basis in truth: Though they go by many different names, mindfulness and other contemplative practices have been present in many different religious and spiritual traditions for centuries. Buddhists have practiced mindfulness for over 2,500 years (Gunaratana, 2012; Rāhula, 1974), and even before that, it has been a common practice for followers of Taoism (Blofeld, 1978; Mikulas, 2011; Zuangzhi, Feng, & English, 2014), Jainism (Bronkhorst, 1986; Kumat, 2007; Mahapragya, 2011; Stuart, 2017), and Hinduism (Brown & Engler, 1980; Dass, 2010; Dreyfus, 2011; Greenberg & Harris, 2012; Tang & Posner, 2013). Mindfulness has been an integral part of the practices of yoga, which literally means "union," for thousands of years (Boccio, 1993; Hartranft, 2003; Salmon, Lush, Jablonski, & Sephton, 2009; Vidyanand, 2007; Yogananda, 1946). Similar practices are also common in Sikhism

(Duggal, 1988; Sangara, 2017; Şenel, 2019), Islam (Ijaz, Khalily, & Ahmad, 2017; Thomas, Furber, & Grey, 2017; Wiguna, Pamungkas, Ningsih, & Hasan, 2018), and among Sufis (Gul & Jahangir, 2019; Helminski, 2017; Isgandarova, 2019; Salyers, 2017).

Growing up in the Christian church, I was once told, "Meditation is evil, because if you open up your mind, the devil will jump in there." In fact, there is some truth in that statement, because when you pause to notice your own mind, you are likely to find all manner of bizarre thoughts that have been there all along but have gone unnoticed. While some might ascribe those thoughts to a malevolent supernatural entity, it may simply be a product of a wide variety of past inputs from society, peers, and movies, and/or the mind just exercising its creative capacity.

Despite what I was told as a child, there is a long history of contemplative practices in many of the Christian traditions (Laird, 2006; Symington & Symington, 2012; Tan, 2011; Tyler, 2018). Brother Lawrence was a 17th-century Christian monk whose writings closely resemble modern mindfulness writings (Claire, 2016). The famous Psalm (46:10) suggests, "Be still, and know that I am God." It is difficult to be in touch with any kind of spiritual experience when one's mind is constantly lost in ruminations and worries.

Reality: Because practices like mindfulness are so often associated with religious practices, a majority of people have mistakenly believed that mindfulness is strictly a religious practice. This is like saying, "If you burn a candle, you are doing a religious practice, because religions burn candles at their ceremonies." A candle is a tool that is used for both religious and secular purposes, to create light and a peaceful atmosphere. Likewise, mindfulness is a tool for developing (or rediscovering) one's ability to be present in the moment. Religions use that tool for spiritual purposes, and others use that tool to become better employees, partners, parents, and citizens.

Because mindfulness can be applied in so many areas of life, we could say there is also a "secular mindfulness." Mindfulness has been well researched as an effective intervention to aid in fostering and maintaining mental and physical health. Martial artists use the practices to aid in being fully present to better manage conflicts and daily life. Airplane pilots use it for situational awareness and decision-making. Business executives use it to reduce burnout and to foster empathy. The list goes on and on.

Ultimately, of course, mindfulness is a tool for breaking free of artificially created limiting constructs to live fully in this present moment, the only time we can ever be. If one were to attempt to put it into words, one could say that there is no real difference in this moment between spiritual and secular, as those distinctions are created by thinking.

Summary: Mindfulness has been a part of spiritual and religious traditions for thousands of years. However, it is not an exclusively religious practice. The practice of mindfulness can be helpful for a wide variety of areas in life, such as work, relationships, and health.

Further Resources

Blofeld, J. (1978). *Taoism—The road to immortality*. Shambhala Publications.

Clair, E. S. (2016). *Bringing mindfulness and Brother Lawrence together: Christian implications for the modern Christian*. Doctoral Dissertation. Biola University.

Dass, R. (2010). *Be here now*. Harmony.

Duggal, K. S. (1988). *Philosophy and faith of Sikhism*. Himalayan Institute Press.

Hartranft, C. (2003). *The Yoga-Sutra of Patanjali: A new translation with commentary*. Shambhala Publications.

Helminski, K. E. (2017). *Living presence (revised): The Sufi path to mindfulness and the essential self*. Penguin.

Mahapragya, A. S. (2011). *Techniques of Prekshadhyan*. Ladnun: Jain Vishwa Bharati.

Rāhula, W. (1974). *What the Buddha taught*. Grove Press.

Tan, S. Y. (2011). Mindfulness and acceptance-based cognitive behavioral therapies: Empirical evidence and clinical applications from a Christian perspective. *Journal of Psychology and Christianity*, *30*(3), 243.

Thomas, J., Furber, S. W., & Grey, I. (2017). The rise of mindfulness and its resonance with the Islamic tradition. *Mental Health, Religion & Culture, 20*(10), 973–985.

Yogananda, P. (1946). *Autobiography of a Yogi*. Self-Realization Fellowship.

Myth: Mindfulness comes from Buddhism. This myth is related to the previous one. Many people believe that mindfulness is strictly a Buddhist practice. I have even seen many scholarly, peer-reviewed journal articles state this as if it were a fact.

Basis in truth: Buddhism was founded over 2,500 years ago by a man named Siddhartha Gautama, who discovered and shared a way of "waking up" to reality in the present moment. He was then called a "Buddha," which means "awakened one." In one of his first public talks, the Buddha laid out an eightfold path to awakening, which includes the practice of mindfulness (Sanskrit: smṛti समृति; Pali: sati सती). The Sanskrit and Pali words for mindfulness mean awareness, presence of mind, or attentiveness to the present moment. Interestingly, they also mean recollection and remembrance, not necessarily in the sense of bringing to mind the past, but to "re-collect" or "re-member" oneself in the present.

In Chinese and Japanese Buddhism, the character for mindfulness is written as 念, which consists of the character for "now" 今 over the character for "mind" or "heart" 心. Hence, we can translate the character for mindfulness as "now mind," or keeping one's heart and mind in the present moment.

Vipassanā (Pāli) or vipaśyanā (Sanskrit विपश्यना), literally "clear seeing," or insight meditation, is a Buddhist practice which uses mindfulness to develop a deeper and visceral understanding of the nature of reality as categorized by the three marks of existence: impermanence, suffering, and lack of inherent self-nature (Gunaratana, 1996; Hart & Goenka, 2019).

Over the centuries, Buddhism developed a detailed and sophisticated, yet simple, structured set of exercises for developing skill in the practice of mindfulness. Early Buddhist texts describe the four foundations of mindfulness practice (Gunaratana, 2012; Sears, 2014; Tirch, Silberstein, & Kolts, 2015).

The first foundation is mindfulness of the body. Even though it is the most "concrete" and physical of the four, it can still be challenging to be aware of the dynamic nature of our physical bodies and to be able to directly perceive through our senses rather than confuse our thoughts and mental images with that physical reality. The second foundation is mindfulness of feelings, which are more subtle than physical sensations, and can generally be noticed as pleasant, unpleasant, and neutral. The third foundation is mindfulness of thoughts, which occur at an even more subtle level. Most people are so close to their thoughts that it is difficult to notice them as thoughts.

The fourth foundation is mindfulness of phenomena. If one pays attention to the ongoing events of reality and existence, one begins to see patterns. Building on the previous three foundations, one can perceive reality much more directly, unfiltered by preconceived ideas and unbiased by conditioned emotional reactions. For example, one begins to see how everything is interconnected, a concept called interdependence. Science has also discovered this. If scientists want to isolate something to study it carefully, they quickly discover that it is practically impossible. If they put a substance in a container, the container might affect it. The substance might be affected by the movement of trucks driving by the lab. The substance may be affected by the temperature of the room and even the warmth of the scientist's body.

Likewise, one can see that all living things, including human beings, cannot be separated from the environment. Our bodies are composed of the food we have transformed. The food came from animals or plants, which grew in sunlight, nurtured in the soil with rain. In that sense, we are connected with the plants, sun, rain, and soil. Having insights like this is one of the reasons why mindfulness is such a useful tool for spiritual awakening for Buddhists.

With so many good Buddhist writings and teachers on the subject of mindfulness, it is understandable that mindfulness is often thought of as strictly a Buddhist practice.

Reality: Many of the early advocates of mindfulness in clinical work, such as Jon Kabat-Zinn (2013), Jack Kornfield (2006), Tara Brach (2004), and Mark Epstein (2009), were trained in Buddhism and/or Zen Buddhism. They took their many years of Buddhist training and worked hard to translate the essence of mindfulness practice into secular and scientific terms in order to help alleviate the suffering of others.

Buddhism teaches many mindfulness practices that were integrated into modern formal mindfulness programs like Mindfulness-Based Stress Reduction (MBSR) (Kabat-Zinn, 2013) and Mindfulness-Based Cognitive Therapy (Segal, Williams, & Teasdale, 2013). These and many other well-researched mindfulness programs commonly utilize exercises like mindful eating, the body scan, mindful breathing, and mindful listening. Of course, anyone can notice their bodies, pay attention to eating one's food, and feeling one's breath. These are obviously not exclusively Buddhist activities.

I too have been extensively trained in Zen and other Buddhist teachings and received full ordination in each of the three major schools of Buddhism: the Theravada (Way of the Elders), Mahayana (Great Vehicle), and Vajrayana (Diamond Vehicle). However, when I do research and clinical work, and help people with problems like stress, anxiety, and depression, I am strictly a clinician. While my background was a useful vehicle for me to practice and discover deep insights about mindfulness, I have found that in my clinical work, everything can be expressed in terms of scientific research.

After all, mindfulness just means paying attention. I obviously have profound respect for and feel a deep connection with Buddhism, but Buddhism is not for everyone. When I read the writings of Buddhist teachings from thousands of years ago, I am amazed at the insights and profundity of what they wrote, but of course, such old writings also sometimes contain superstitious thinking that was a product of cultural influences and lack of scientific awareness. Fascinatingly, I once heard the Dalai Lama say that if science contradicts the teachings of Buddhism, he will change what he teaches.

When I am with my Zen friends, I enjoy donning robes and engaging in practices that link us with a 2,500-year-old tradition. However, I am even more at home in my psychotherapy office guiding people through their psychological distress with concrete and practical tools that include mindfulness exercises. Applying a scientific and practical approach to mindfulness to people who are not interested in the teachings of Buddhism does not take anything away from those who do practice Buddhism.

The word "science" comes from Latin and means "to know." At its best, science is a quest to discover the empirical truth, which means to observe and experience reality through the senses, aside from theories and conceptualizations. This is precisely what mindfulness is all about, and the world desperately needs more of this in modern times.

Summary: Buddhism developed and honed a variety of mindfulness practices for being present in the moment to a high degree. Many early mindfulness advocates in recent times had a background in Buddhist training, but given that mindfulness simply means paying attention, it does not belong to Buddhism or any other tradition. The essential principles of mindfulness can be learned and experienced through science in a practical and secular way.

Further Resources

Brach, T. (2004). *Radical acceptance: Embracing your life with the heart of a Buddha*. Bantam Books.

Epstein, M. (2009). *Going on being: Life at the crossroads of Buddhism and psychotherapy*. Simon and Schuster.

Gunaratana, B. H. (1996). *Mindfulness in plain English, revised and expanded edition*. Wisdom Publications.

Gunaratana, H. (2012). *The four foundations of mindfulness in plain English*. Simon and Schuster.

Hart, W., & Goenka, S. N. (2019). *The art of living: Vipassana meditation as taught by SN Goenka*. Embassy Books.

Kornfield, J. (2006). *Mindfulness, bliss, and beyond: A meditator's handbook*. Simon and Schuster.

Sears, R. (2014). *Mindfulness: Living through challenges and enriching your life in this moment*. London, UK: Wiley-Blackwell.

Tirch, D., Silberstein, L. R., & Kolts, R. L. (2015). *Buddhist psychology and cognitive-behavioral therapy: A clinician's guide*. Guilford Publications.

Myth: If you are not practicing the full ethical code of Buddhism, you are not doing real mindfulness. Many mindfulness teachers who received their training in the Buddhist tradition believe that pulling mindfulness out of its spiritual context makes it ineffective at best and harmful at worst.

Basis in truth: As discussed in a previous myth, Buddhists have been practicing mindfulness for over 2,500 years. Along with the practice of mindfulness, those who formally consider themselves to be Buddhist agree to take precepts (Mikulas, 2015; Saddhatissa, 1997; Wonji, 2007b), which are ethical guidelines for behavior. Lay Buddhists typically receive the following five precepts:

> The First Precept: I vow to support all living creatures, and refrain from killing.
>
> The Second Precept: I vow to respect the property of others, and refrain from stealing.
>
> The Third Precept: I vow to regard all beings with respect and dignity, and refrain from objectifying others.
>
> The Fourth Precept: I vow to be truthful, and refrain from lying.
>
> The Fifth Precept: I vow to maintain a clear mind, and refrain from harming myself or others with intoxication.

If one wishes to become a teacher, priest, or monk, one is expected to take more and more precepts. In Buddhism, these precepts are not seen as inviolable rules enforced from a supernatural authority. They are seen as expedient means to facilitate becoming more awake. Breaking a precept does not invoke divine punishment but tends to lead one away from the path of awakening. Someone who kills, takes advantage of others, lies, and steals will create chaos in their community and is not going to be able to concentrate or practice mindfulness. Becoming intoxicated makes it difficult to pay attention, wake up, and be present in the moment.

In Zen Buddhism, the goal is to let go of the teachings, seeing them as expedient means, like a raft used for crossing the river. After you have crossed the river, you do not need to carry the raft around. However, you should not throw the raft away before you cross the river. Likewise, I have seen many people interested in Zen who throw away the teachings before they have worked through them.

In the same way that Buddhist teachers take precepts, mental health professionals like psychologists agree to abide by their ethical codes and laws. In learning about human psychology and how to motivate change, in a certain sense, psychologists are learning how to manipulate people, and the people who come to see them can be in a very vulnerable state.

Many professions and disciplines have ethical codes. The martial art I practice, To-Shin Do, based on the arts of the ninja (Hayes, 2012), has a 14-point Code of Mindful Action. It serves as a model for mindful behavior when learning the art of self-defense. While most students are motivated to learn the art for self-protection, health, and understanding the mind, the techniques of the martial arts of course have the potential for misuse.

Mindfulness is a tool for learning to be present and pay attention. Tools like hammers can be used to create works of beauty or can be used to smash things. There are some very real potential dangers in taking up mindfulness practice (Britton, 2019; Kostanski & Hassed, 2008; Sears & Chard, 2016). One is from so-called mindfulness teachers who are actually only teaching to aggrandize themselves, making claims to having some kind of secret, inside information. As in psychotherapy, talking to people about their struggles can lead to a sense of emotional intimacy that can be used for selfish gain by unscrupulous individuals.

Another potential danger is that if people rigidly believe that they should always be accepting and nonjudgmental, it can allow injustices to continue in the world.

Yet another serious potential problem arises when mindfulness is used to try to get rid of thoughts and emotions. For someone struggling with certain mental health disorders like anxiety, avoidance tends to exacerbate the anxiety, creating a vicious spiral of struggle as anxiety about anxiety builds on itself. Also, those with deeply buried traumatic issues may open up a flood of flashbacks and emotions if they do not know how to work with those experiences in a skillful way.

If your goal is spiritual awakening, having mentors, teachings, and ethical codes from a structured approach like Buddhism can be very helpful to guide you through these and other potential pitfalls.

Reality: Concern about misuse of mindfulness is warranted. However, not everyone agrees on a universal ethical code, and the potential for misuse is not a reason to withhold teaching mindfulness to only a select few.

Given that mindfulness is simply paying attention, one might argue the world needs much more noticing. If people are truly more aware of their thoughts, feelings, behaviors, and their impact on other people, they will naturally tend to become more considerate of how they interact with others.

In fact, brain scan research on mindfulness shows a volume increase in the medial prefrontal cortex (mPFC) (Lazar, Kerr, Wasserman, Gray, Greve, et al., 2005). The functions of the mPFC include empathy, self-awareness, and morality (Siegel, 2007). There have indeed been quite a few studies connecting mindfulness practice with empathy (Gür & Yilmaz, 2020; Jones, Bodie, & Hughes, 2019; Kemper & Khirallah, 2015; Kingsbury, 2009; Trent, Park, Bercovitz, & Chapman, 2016; Walsh, 2008).

While ethics codes can be very useful, they are an "outside-in" approach. That is, external guidelines help to foster an internal experience over time. Mindfulness can be considered an "inside-out" approach. If you practice mindfulness and become more aware of your own thoughts and feelings, increasingly notice the impact you have on others, and recognize that you need others and the world around you, you will naturally discover how interconnected everything really is. You will therefore be more disposed to treat other beings and the environment as aspects of yourself.

Of course, it would be naive to think no one will attempt to misuse mindfulness. Some people have clinical personality disorders, characterized by an inability to be aware of and monitor their own behavior (Lester, 2018). Brain scans of these individuals show deficits in the areas of the brain related to empathy and self-monitoring (Nenadic, Güllmar, Dietzek, Langbein, Steinke, & Gaser, 2015; O'Neill & Frodl, 2012; Quattrini, Pini, Pievani, Magni, Lanfredi, et al., 2019; Raine, Lencz, Bihrle, LaCasse, et al., 2000; Smesny, Große, Gussew, Langbein, Schönfeld, et al., 2018). Such individuals are not likely to want to follow ethical codes created by other people anyway, since it is difficult for them to see any perspective other than their own as valid. However, in my experience, such people are not likely to stick with mindfulness training though it is very helpful if they do.

Interestingly, I have found this true in other areas of my like, like martial arts, clinical psychology, and Zen training. Even though some people may misuse the skills they acquire in those disciplines, it is still valuable to offer these concepts and principles to the public to help the people who need them. It also seems mysterious how people without ethics tend not to stick with the training long term. Perhaps it is because progress in so many areas of life depends on self-reflection and ability to absorb feedback.

While a code of ethics can be helpful for many people, I cannot imagine a universal ethical code that would work for everyone. Who gets to decide what is correct behavior? How would these codes account for changing times and scientific advances? How could it attend to cultural and other diversity issues? How would these codes be reinforced? Since mindfulness is simply paying attention in the present moment, how could one say only they have the "real" mindfulness practice?

Summary: If your goal is spiritual awakening, having mentors and teachings from a structured approach like Buddhism or another spiritual or secular tradition can be very helpful. However, anyone can benefit from practicing mindfulness to help them through the challenges of daily life and to enrich their moments. Mindfulness is a tool for paying attention. Like any tool, it can be used in ways that cause harm, and it can also help to alleviate suffering.

Further Resources

Britton, W. B. (2019). Can mindfulness be too much of a good thing? The value of a middle way. *Current Opinion in Psychology, 28*, 159–165.

Lazar, S. W., Kerr, C. E., Wasserman, R. H., Gray, J. R., Greve, D. N., Treadway, M. T., . . . Fischl, B. (2005). Meditation experience is associated with increased cortical thickness. *Neuroreport, 16*(17), 1893–1897.

Mikulas, W. L. (2015). Ethics in Buddhist training. *Mindfulness, 6*(1), 14–16.

Siegel, D. J. (2007). *The mindful brain: Reflection and attunement in the cultivation of well-being (Norton series on interpersonal neurobiology)*. WW Norton & Company.

Walsh, R. A. (2008). Mindfulness and empathy. In S. F. Hick & T. Bien (Eds.), *Mindfulness and the therapeutic relationship*, pp. 72–86.

Wonji (2007). *Buddhist precepts: A guide for western Buddhist Lay practitioners*. Buddha Dharma University Press.

Myth: Mindfulness practice makes you a Zen master. Some people believe mindfulness practice is all about achieving some spiritual attainment, like becoming a Zen master. People also have a lot of misconceptions about what Zen is all about.

Basis in truth: A Zen master is someone who has experienced "awakening," having woken up from the artificial realities created by the realm of thinking (An, 1975; Sears, 2017a; Watts, 1957; Wonji Dharma, 2011). The Chinese and Japanese character for enlightenment or awakening is 悟, which literally translates as "perceive, realize, discern, or understand." The portion of the character on the left is an abbreviation of 心, which means "heart/mind." In the upper right corner is the character 五, meaning "five." The bottom right is 口,

20

which means "mouth" or opening, referring to the senses. Hence, the entire character implies the mind and five senses in harmony, or the mind clearly perceiving through the five senses.

Hence, to be awake is to clearly perceive reality in the present moment through the five senses. My Zen teacher Wonji Dharma's teacher, Seung Sahn, defined Zen practice as paying attention to what you see, hear, smell, taste, and feel, moment after moment after moment. This is a perfect definition of mindfulness.

One of the pioneers of mindfulness, Jon Kabat-Zinn (2005), was also a student of Zen Master Seung Sahn, and his Zen training heavily influenced his practice and understanding of mindfulness.

Reality: While its goal is to have direct realization and to let go of attachment to fixed beliefs, Zen is a school of Buddhism. Mindfulness is a tool used in Zen, but practicing mindfulness is not necessarily about becoming a Zen master. You do not have to be a Zen master to clearly perceive reality in the present moment through the five senses. All human beings have experienced this and can do so at any moment.

There are a lot of myths as to what a Zen master really is. Zen masters are not without feeling. Many people mistakenly use the word Zen as meaning "chill" or emotionless. In Zen, such a person is described as a "stone Buddha," because if you have no feelings, you are no different than a rock (Watts, 1957). Our feelings give us inspiration, motivation, and compassion. True Zen masters have a rich emotional life but do not get as easily stuck in their feelings. Fear arises and falls, but there is less fear of being afraid. Sadness comes and goes, but they do not get depressed about feeling sad.

Also, Zen masters do not have blank minds. They have simply changed their relationships to their thoughts. They see thoughts as thoughts, as mental phenomena, not as reality. Confusing thoughts with the realities they represent is a source of endless confusion and struggle.

I have met many individuals who have been given the title of Zen master. The schools of Zen have splintered into many diverse spiritual organizations. As with all spiritual organizations composed of human beings, it is difficult to avoid issues of ego, power, and politics. I have met Zen masters who are truly awake, compassionate people. I have also met "Zen masters" who use the title to further their own egos, and hence reinforce their own separateness, still lost in the realm of thinking as they create more chaos in the world.

My own teacher gave me transmission as a Zen master, and I am definitely not always mindful. Old conditionings and habits patterns can become deeply ingrained in the human mind. However, I have begun to let go of "trying" to be mindful. I have increasingly recognized that I cannot be anywhere but the present. In this moment, I am feeling grateful for our connection as I share these words with you.

Summary: Zen students use mindfulness as one tool for coming into the present moment. However, people have many reasons for formally practicing mindfulness, and very few people are interested in studying Zen, which is a school of Buddhism. In any case, Zen masters are still human beings with feelings. This reminds me of an old joke: What is the difference between a Zen master and an ordinary person? An ordinary person thinks there is a difference.

Further Resources

An, T. T. (1975). *Zen philosophy, Zen practice*. Dharma Publishing.

Kabat-Zinn, J. (2005). *Coming to our senses: Healing ourselves and the world through mindfulness*. Hachette UK.

Sears, R. (2017). *The sense of self: Perspectives from science and Zen Buddhism*. New York: Springer Nature.

Watts, A. (1957). *The way of Zen*. New York: Pantheon.

Wonji Dharma. (2011). *Wu Shan Lu five mountain record*. Buddha Dharma University Press.

2 Myths about What Mindfulness Is

Given the popularity of mindfulness in recent decades, very diverse opinions have arisen as to exactly what mindfulness is. Even though I make part of my living through teaching and writing about mindfulness, I am beginning to tire of hearing that word so overused. The word is being tacked on to thousands of things, very often in inappropriate and misleading ways, and is sometimes even taught in ways that cause harm. In this chapter, we will explore the myths people have about what mindfulness is.

Myth: <u>Mindfulness makes you feel better.</u> One of the many reasons people practice mindfulness is that they want to feel better. They are suffering, and they want relief from their suffering.

Basis in truth: I once consulted with a neurology research team who was trying to see if lowering stress would lower the frequency of seizures among individuals with epilepsy. Before they could implement their intervention, they needed to establish a baseline for how stressed each individual was. In order to do this, they gave everyone a pager and paged them several times a day for a few days. Interestingly, their stress began going down even before the "intervention" could be given. It turned out that the act of pausing to check in with themselves throughout the day lowered their stress. This makes perfect sense from a mindfulness perspective. People are often spinning in their minds, pushing down their emotions, and tensing up their bodies as they move through life. When they pause to notice, they may start to recognize these patterns.

Just as muddy water settles when left alone, sometimes our internal struggles can subside when we pause to pay attention.

It's like watching a scary movie that has you worried, scared, and tense. When you hit the pause button, and check in with yourself, you might decide it is no longer necessary to hold on to any of that muscle tension. Likewise, it is easy to get lost in the movies in our minds, and get anxious and tense about our imagined future problems and bygone past issues. When we pause to check in, the present moment is often not as bad as our minds make things out to be.

Reality: People who practice mindfulness often do feel better during and after a mindfulness exercise, which of course is quite wonderful. However, sometimes people attempt to use mindfulness to avoid unpleasant feelings, which tends to increase struggle. Struggling with or trying to get rid of strong emotions sometimes works temporarily but tends to set up long-term cycles of struggle (Leahy, Tirch, & Napolitano, 2011; Harris, 2008; Hayes, 2020a; Sears, 2021). After all, since your thoughts and feelings come from yourself, struggling with them is like having a tug of war with your own two hands. It only wears you out.

Interestingly, research has shown that people who try to get rid of negative emotions also tend to have less ability to feel positive emotions (Hayes, 2020a). The attempt to avoid unpleasant feelings can inadvertently turn into discomfort with all feelings.

Mindfulness is about noticing and embracing reality as it is (Kabat-Zinn, 2013). Because people have a tendency to live in their heads, they develop a habit of being unaware of what they are feeling emotionally and in their bodies. When you consciously choose to notice, you may not necessarily like what you find. You may become more aware of all the negative thoughts swirling around, all the unpleasant emotions churning, and all the physical discomforts present in your body. However, if they are there, they are already there anyway. Ignoring them tends not to be a very good long-term strategy. Noticing is an important first step in proactively taking care of yourself. How can you make wise and healthy choices if you are not even aware of what is going on inside yourself?

Of course, once you become aware of discomfort, you might choose to do something about it. If you pay attention and notice you have a headache, you are "feeling worse," but then might choose to go take an aspirin. Also, paying attention to the early signs of problems can help to prevent further trouble down the road. If you notice that you are feeling thirsty from dehydration, or you notice a buildup of muscle tension in the shoulders, you can get a drink or stretch your shoulders to prevent a headache, even though noticing the thirst and the muscle tension makes you feel "worse" in the moment.

Though subtle, there is a big difference between noticing and acknowledging unpleasant emotions, then choosing to do a self-care activity, and trying not to notice the unpleasant emotions by distracting yourself from them. In the latter case, the desire to get rid of the emotion can inadvertently create struggle with the emotion. After all, if it is your own emotion, any struggle to avoid it or get rid of it is a struggle with yourself. If you acknowledge the emotion as a messenger, you can accept the message for what it is, then make a conscious choice about how to respond (Teasdale, Williams, & Segal, 2014).

Over time, you can begin to internalize the habit of allowing emotions to flow naturally, and hence will feel "better" compared to times in your life when old habits of struggle kept emotions stuck in a spiraling pattern. You will still feel anxious when potential danger approaches, sad when you lose a loved one, and feel pain when you are injured, but you will be less anxious about anxiety, less sad about grieving, and not add as much suffering on top of your pain.

Summary: In the spirit of Acceptance and Commitment Therapy (ACT) (Hayes, 2005; Hayes, Strosahl, & Wilson, 2012), we could say that mindfulness is about *feeling* better, rather than feeling *better*. Mindfulness is about checking in with reality as it is. There are times when practicing mindfulness allows you to let go of unnecessary struggle, and therefore leads to a sense of feeling better. At other times, you may check in and notice more distressing thoughts, unpleasant emotions, and uncomfortable sensations than you thought you had. In any case, it is usually better to be aware of reality as it is if you are going to manage it skillfully.

Further Resources

Leahy, R. L., Tirch, D., & Napolitano, L. A. (2011). *Emotion regulation in psychotherapy: A practitioner's guide.* Guilford Press.

Harris, R. (2008). *The happiness trap: How to stop struggling and start living.* Trumpeter.

Hayes, S. C. (2005). *Get out of your mind and into your life: The new acceptance and commitment therapy.* New Harbinger Publications.

Hayes, S. C. (2020). *A liberated mind: How to pivot toward what matters.* Avery.

Sears, R. (2021). *ACT with anxiety: An acceptance and commitment therapy workbook to get you unstuck from anxiety and enrich your life.* Eau Claire, WI: PESI Publishing & Media, Inc.

Teasdale, J., Williams, M., & Segal, Z. (2014). *The mindful way workbook: An 8-week program to free yourself from depression and emotional distress.* New York: Guilford Press.

Myth: Mindfulness makes you feel worse. There are people who begin to practice mindfulness but give up immediately, because they say it makes them feel worse, bringing up all kinds of negative thoughts and emotions that they do not want to experience. Their attitude is that it is better to just plod along through life and not open up a can of negative cognitive and emotional worms.

Basis in truth: As discussed in the previous myth, because many people try to ignore or suppress negative thoughts and emotions, when they pause to pay attention, they may not have noticed all the underlying unpleasant things going on in their minds, emotions, and bodies, and hence they will believe they now feel "worse" (Sears, 2017b).

This is especially true for those who have experienced very difficult events, like grief or posttraumatic stress disorder (PTSD). If you have had a traumatic experience, and you try not to remember the event, and try to suppress your feelings, they may come up strongly when you begin to pay attention. Likewise, if you have lost a loved one, it can be painful to notice thoughts and memories about them, and the grief feelings can seem overwhelming at times.

Even in daily life without extreme trauma, modern-day society can impose a lot of pressure on people to take care of their bills, perform well in a busy work environment, and manage all the chaos that goes along with having a family. For many people, the answer to dealing with all of this is to keep pushing on toward an imagined future when everything will be better, and they never have time to stop and process all of those feelings of stress.

Because many individuals do not want to feel those kinds of strong underlying emotions, they feel like they are stuck between a rock and a hard place. Trying not to feel is hard, but feeling directly seems harder, so they choose to push down their feelings, even though they still manage to erupt at times anyway.

If the thoughts and feelings are already there, or just below the surface, and your habit has been to suppress them, it can definitely feel like paying attention to them will make things worse.

Reality: All human beings have a wide range of emotions and thoughts. Our moods and thinking patterns can change from day to day and even moment to moment. If you feel worse when you are paying attention, chances are, those experiences were already there anyway.

Trying not to think about something is already thinking about it. Trying not to feel something is adding struggle to your emotions. Ignoring physical pain may be necessary at times, but sometimes pain can give us important information. If we pay attention, we may feel worse in that moment, but these thoughts, emotions, and sensations can be barometers to let us know how we are doing. Through mindfulness practice, we can change our relationship to these unpleasant experiences. A thought that life is not worth living indicates you are getting overwhelmed or depressed. A strong emotion tells you that something important is happening. Pushing away pain can be helpful in the short run, and sometimes even necessary during a flare-up, but it becomes exhausting if you try to keep it up all the time.

I suffered a neck injury, and at first, I was very annoyed with the pain. While it was not easy, I learned to relate to the pain as a messenger. Rather than pushing it away, I began feeling compassion for my body. The pain was often giving me information about the need to change my lifestyle, and sometimes it was a reminder to do my exercises more often.

Because of the potential for things to seem worse when you become aware of them, mindfulness is sometimes discouraged. When you stop distracting yourself with busy thoughts about other times and places, you are likely to find all kinds of random thoughts moving through your mind. You will likely never even know where those thoughts are coming from or why they are there. Such thoughts are often simply the creative firings of old brain pathways, based on memories of past experiences (Carlson & Birkett, 2021; Torneke, 2010).

This potential for things to get worse before they get better is known as the "extinction burst" and comes up frequently in raising children. Have you ever had the experience of waiting in the checkout line of a grocery store with a toddler? While waiting in line, your toddler is standing there with empty hands and nothing to do, and the shiny chocolate bar wrappers sitting there at toddler's-eye level start to look pretty attractive. The child may pick up a candy bar and say, "I want a chocolate bar!"

Being a responsible adult, you say, "No Honey, put that back, we're about to eat supper."

Not so easily dissuaded, the toddler says, "But I REALLY want a chocolate bar!!!"

Now, if you are fairly consistent with your child, and you always mean what you say, they may still ask, and they may still whine. But the worst possible thing you can do is give in every now and then after the behavior ramps up. After saying no twice, the child may decide to start loudly chanting, "I WANT A CHOCOLATE BAR! I WANT A CHOCOLATE BAR!" Suddenly, the entire grocery store is staring at you, wondering what kind of parent you must be if you cannot control your own child. If to avoid embarrassment, you suddenly say, "Fine! Take your chocolate bar!", you just reinforced that whiny behavior.

Later, you might regret that you gave in, so you decide to do what the therapy books tell you to do (Barkley & Benton, 2013; Phelan, 2010). You decide to be consistent, like a broken record, like a robot without emotion. When the toddler gets to the loud chanting, you stay firm in your denial of the chocolate bar. You know what is likely to happen? The toddler will probably start screaming at the top of their lungs, or lay on the floor and pound their fists in a temper tantrum.

I once worked with a mother who did not give her toddler baths very often. She said that once she put her daughter in the bathtub, she would not want to stop playing with her bath toys. Even after an hour, when the water had long become cold, the girl would scream and throw a tantrum when the mother would tell her to get out of the bathtub, so the mother let her play longer, reinforcing the tantrums. The mother's plan was to simply not give the girl baths very often rather than deal with the tantrums.

These phenomena are the behavioral manifestations of the extinction burst (Miltenberger, 2012; Wolpe, 1990). When you finally decide to set boundaries, and to be consistent and firm, the behavior will likely get worse before it gets better.

This extinction burst process will also happen with emotions like anxiety when practicing mindfulness (VanElzakker, Dahlgreen, Davis, Dubois, & Shin, 2014; Sears, 2021). This is why super intelligent people can go their whole lives with anxiety. When they finally move into it, and allow themselves to feel it, it gets worse, and because they are intelligent, they go back to avoidance, because they do not want to feel the anxiety. Unfortunately, this keeps them trapped in a cycle of struggle.

It is very important to be aware of the extinction burst, as it applies to distressing thoughts, unpleasant emotions, uncomfortable sensations, and unhealthy habits. Otherwise, when you do what you need to do, and notice it is getting worse, you may think avoidance is better. If you know it may get worse ahead of time, you can take some comfort in knowing that you are doing it right if it gets a little worse at first.

Through mindfulness training, people can develop kindness and self-compassion for their experiences, even the unpleasant ones (Neff, 2003; Paulson, Huggins, & Gentile, 2019; Tirch, Schoendorff, & Silberstein, 2014). This opens up room to work with difficult experiences in a conscious, more skillful way.

Summary: Because people often have a tendency to ignore or suppress uncomfortable thoughts, emotions, and feelings, they can become trapped in a cycle of struggle with their own experiences. Bringing attention to them through mindful awareness can make a person feel worse. This phenomenon is known as the extinction burst. However, through mindfulness practice, one can come to relate to even unpleasant internal events as messengers, providing important information. Being present even when things seem to be getting worse allows one to break the cycle of struggle and unhelpful reactions in order to take proactive steps toward self-care.

Further Resources

Barkley, R. A., & Benton, C. M. (2013). *Your defiant child: Eight steps to better behavior*. Guilford Press.

Carlson, N. R., & Birkett, M. A. (2021). *Physiology of behavior*, 13th edition. Pearson.

Sears, R. (2017). *The cognitive-behavioral therapy and mindfulness toolbox*. Eau Claire, WI: PESI Publishing & Media, Inc.

Tirch, D., Schoendorff, B., & Silberstein, L. R. (2014). *The ACT practitioner's guide to the science of compassion: Tools for fostering psychological flexibility*. New Harbinger Publications.

Torneke, N. (2010). *Learning RFT: An introduction to relational frame theory and its clinical application*. New Harbinger Publications.

VanElzakker, M. B., Dahlgren, M. K., Davis, F. C., Dubois, S., & Shin, L. M. (2014). From Pavlov to PTSD: The extinction of conditioned fear in rodents, humans, and anxiety disorders. *Neurobiology of Learning and Memory, 113*, 3–18. doi:10.1016/j.nlm.2013.11.014 PMID 24321650.

Wolpe, J. (1990). *The practice of behavior therapy*. Pergamon Press.

<u>Myth: Mindfulness is about thinking positive.</u> Because our minds are often filled with worries and ruminations, some people associate mindfulness with uplifting sayings and happy thoughts. They attempt to use mindfulness to get rid of negative thoughts and replace them with positive ones.

Basis in truth: Decades of research studies have shown that the brain appears to be hardwired to look for what might go wrong, thus giving us a negativity bias (Norris, 2021; Rozin & Royzman, 2001; Unkelbach, Alves, & Koch, 2020). This certainly makes sense from an evolutionary perspective. If I consider all animals as potentially deadly, I will be cautious around them all. There may be times I encounter a friendly animal, but if I am cautious and avoid it, no harm is done. On the other hand, if I were to naturally think positive about all animals, even though I might get joy from befriending some of them, it only takes one fierce or poisonous animal to kill me. In that case, my genes are not passed on to the next generation. In this sense, a negativity bias appears to provide a selective advantage, as only those who were more likely to look for the negative were able to survive.

Another effect of this negativity bias is forgetting about positive things once they are obtained. Once you have enough food, you focus on where the next threat might come from. Once you have a secure place to live, you focus on finding a mate. In order to survive, you set aside things that are going well and focus on the next potential danger.

However, with the conveniences and relative safety we experience in modern times, life is not as pleasant when we are continuously thinking about and looking for what might go wrong. What is the point of surviving to survive? Mindfulness is about recognizing thoughts as representations of reality, and thus can help us break free from this automatic tendency to overly focus on thoughts of what might go wrong. When we are no longer as caught up in negative thinking, we can develop more appreciation for the positive, for what we have to be thankful for in our lives.

Mindfulness can also serve as a tool to help us develop clarity about our values and what we want our lives to be about. When we are better able to be aware of our thoughts, we can separate out old unhelpful automatic messages and set clear intentions to engage in the activities that are important to us. Thinking clearly about what you want from life is an essential first step to making it happen.

Reality: Mindfulness is about noticing thoughts, not necessarily about changing thoughts. For some people, trying to make themselves think positive immediately creates more negative thoughts.

Take, for example, the research on affirmations. The idea is to clarify and say out loud something you want to believe about yourself. The purpose is to undo previous negative programming by continuing to say these things to yourself until you believe them. Many individuals have found this helpful to program themselves to think in new ways more in line with their values.

Positive affirmations can be helpful for someone who already has high self-esteem, but for many people they can backfire and make them feel worse (Wood, Elaine Perunovic, & Lee, 2009). In the classic Saturday Night Live skit, would-be therapist Stuart Smalley would say, "I'm good enough, I'm smart enough, and doggone it, people like me." Yet, halfway through the show, something stressful would happen, spawning a cascade of negative thoughts about being a failure, that people hated him, and that his show would be cancelled.

Therapists have used cognitive behavioral therapy (CBT) for decades, which originally focused on changing one's mood by changing one's thinking (Burns & Beck, 1999; Greenberger & Padesky, 2015). Positive thoughts tend to be correlated with positive moods, and negative thoughts tend to be correlated with negative moods. The original idea of CBT was to challenge negative thoughts and replace them with more positive thoughts, or at least more realistic or more helpful ones.

To facilitate this process, clients are given homework assignments like "thought records." First, they write about a situation that was distressing, like dropping and breaking a cup. Then, they write down the thoughts they had, like, "I so stupid and clumsy, I can't do anything right." Next, they notice how that thought made them feel, like angry and depressed. Then, they consider what a more realistic or helpful thought would have been, like, "Everyone has accidents. It doesn't mean I'm stupid or clumsy." Next, they consider what emotion would likely come with that thought, like perhaps only feeling a little frustrated.

CBT is quite popular among psychotherapists and has helped countless individuals. However, sometimes challenging thoughts makes them worse, giving them more power by creating even more argumentation inside their heads. In the above example, after thinking, "Everyone has accidents. It doesn't mean I'm stupid or clumsy," the next thought might be, "Yeah, but I have a lot more accidents than most people because I'm stupid and clumsy." When someone is really caught up in distressing thoughts, these thought battles can go on endlessly, creating increasing stress, anxiety, or depression.

Research in the past couple of decades has shown that while CBT is indeed helpful for a lot of people, it does not work for the reasons originally hypothesized. It turns out that challenging thoughts is not even necessary for CBT to be successful (Longmore & Worrell, 2007).

What seems to be implicit in traditional CBT approaches, but is made more explicit in "third wave," or process-based CBT approaches (Hayes & Hoffman, 2018), is a process known as decentering or defusion (Hayes, Strosahl, & Wilson, 2012; Piaget, 1950; Piaget & Morf, 1958; Segal, Williams, & Teasdale, 2013). When most people think, they feel as if they are "fused" to their thoughts, or as if they are inside the center of their thoughts. Hence these thoughts are conditioned with all kinds of emotions and memories. While it may sound like semantics, experientially, there is a big difference between "I am a loser" and "I am having a thought that I am a loser." In the latter case,

33

one recognizes the thought for what it is—a mental phenomenon, and not literally the reality it is intended to represent.

A movie theater analogy is often used in mindfulness practice to help understand this decentering process (Hayes, Strosahl, & Wilson, 2012; Segal, Williams, & Teasdale, 2013). One of the reasons we go to the movies is to get lost in another world. In the movie theater, we laugh, we cry, we get angry, and we feel afraid, even though we are looking at nothing but images on a screen and are only listening to digital representations of sounds. Likewise, we can get so lost in thoughts that we forget they are only verbal and visual representations of reality. They have no inherent reality outside of the mind. If we step to the back of a movie theater, and get perspective on what is happening, it is easier to remember that what we are witnessing on the movie screen is not really happening. Likewise, if we "step back" from our thoughts, and recognize them as thoughts, we can make room for these thoughts and see them from a broader perspective. We can then choose consciously if we want to interact with these thoughts or refocus on something more important in that moment.

Struggling with our own thoughts, and trying to replace one thought with another, only adds more emotion to these mental representations. A metaphor often used in mindfulness practice is to experience your thoughts as clouds. You cannot fight or push away a cloud, and you cannot hold on to a cloud. The clouds themselves are simply signs of the weather—sunny and clear or cloudy and stormy. Similarly, our thoughts are often signs of our emotional state.

Hence, negative thoughts are not our enemies. They are barometers that give us information about how we are feeling. When our thoughts give us negative views of ourselves, of our world, and of our future, we are likely feeling depressed. When our thoughts are frantic, we are likely anxious.

Our thoughts may provide very useful information at times, warning us to be careful or helping us learn from past mistakes. Sometimes our thoughts are merely old echoes of obsolete programming, no longer useful in our current situation. Our thoughts can sometimes be very helpful advisors, but they make terrible dictators. When we see thoughts for what they are, we can use thoughts as we choose instead of being dominated by them.

Interestingly, thought patterns do tend to change over time. If you no longer fight and struggle with them, negative thoughts tend to become less powerful, because they are not being reinforced. If you practice noticing and appreciating things, your brain pathways will change over time.

Summary: Mindfulness is not about forcing yourself to think positive. Mindfulness practice is about noticing and investigating the true nature of thoughts. In a sense, thoughts are neither positive nor negative; they are simply mental phenomena rising and falling. They can be useful barometers of how you are feeling. Sometimes they are attempts to help us solve problems, and sometimes they are old messages that are no longer helpful. By noticing thoughts as thoughts, we develop the freedom to choose our actions based on what we value, and we break free from the tyranny of thinking.

Further Resources

Burns, D. D., & Beck, A. T. (1999). *Feeling good: The new mood therapy.* Harper Publications.

Greenberger, D., & Padesky, C. A. (2015). *Mind over mood: Change how you feel by changing the way you think.* Guilford Publications.

Hayes, S. C., & Hofmann, S. G. (Eds.). (2018). *Process-based CBT: The science and core clinical competencies of cognitive behavioral therapy.* New Harbinger Publications.

Hayes, S. C., Strosahl, K., & Wilson, K. G. (2012). *Acceptance and commitment therapy: The process and practice of mindful change,* 2nd edition. New York: Guilford Press.

Longmore, R., & Worrell, M. (2007). Do we need to challenge thoughts in cognitive behavior therapy? *Clinical Psychology Review, 27,* 173–187.

Norris, C. J. (2021). The negativity bias, revisited: Evidence from neuroscience measures and an individual differences approach. *Social Neuroscience, 16*(1), 68–82.

Segal, Z., Williams, M., & Teasdale, J. (2013). *Mindfulness-based cognitive therapy for depression*, 2nd edition. New York: Guilford Press.

Wood, J. V., Elaine Perunovic, W. Q., & Lee, J. W. (2009). Positive self-statements: Power for some, Peril for others. *Psychological Science, 20*(7), 860–866. https://doi.org/10.1111/j.1467-9280.2009.02370.x

Myth: Mindfulness makes you happy. There is a lot of stress and suffering in the world, especially in our fast-paced, modern times. Many people think that mindfulness is something that is supposed to make them happy.

Basis in truth: Many ancient spiritual traditions have noted that desire is the root of suffering (Rāhula, 1974; Tirch, Silberstein, & Kolts, 2015). By definition, desire is wanting something you do not have. It involves comparing this moment and what we have to other moments and/or to what others have. Since mindfulness practice emphasizes the suspension of automatic, compulsive judgments, and resting in this moment to appreciate things as they are, the sense of suffering can be reduced, facilitating more of a sense of happiness.

As mentioned in the previous myth, our minds also have a tendency to focus on potential future problems and tend to ignore what is going well. While this has survival value, it can lead to a chronic state of stress and anxiety. Because mindfulness is about being present and noticing, it can lead to a sense of appreciation and gratitude for what we have. Fostering gratitude for what we have does tend to increase happiness (Emmons, 2007, 2008; McCullough, Tsang, & Emmons, 2004).

For example, if you take a few moments right now to think about all the mistakes you have made in the past, all the things on your to-do list, all the potential problems that might happen to you in the future, and how much better certain other people like billionaires have it, you are likely to begin feeling stressed or depressed. If you think of all the things you do have, and how much better off you are compared to the worst times in your life, you are more likely to feel happy.

As I write this, the world is in the midst of a global pandemic. Many people are feeling miserable about the restrictions being placed upon us to reduce the spread of the disease. However, I feel appreciative when I think about my mother, who was a small child in Germany during World War II. Her father went off to a war he did not want to fight and bled to death on the battlefield. She heard bombs drop from the sky and watched her home burn to the ground. Yet, she talked about how grateful she was to be able to eat one egg once a week, and she would often tell me of how happy she felt when the U.S. soldiers gave her chocolate when their tanks came rolling through. When I think about that, and all the other things she went through, and pay attention to all the things and people I have in my life right now, I feel grateful and happy to have a safe place to live and plenty of food to eat.

Reality: Mindfulness is noticing things as they are. Chasing happiness tends to increase our sense of struggle, because ups and downs of emotions are inevitable in life (Harris, 2008). Emotions give us information and motivation in our lives, and they change based on our life circumstances, what is happening in the world, and a myriad of other factors beyond our control. It is impossible to always be happy, and in fact, undesirable. You would not want to be happy if a relative died. It would be natural and appropriate to feel sad. Exhortations to "look at the bright side" or "appreciate those who are still living" are of little consolation when you are grieving.

In fact, you would not know what happiness is if you had not experienced suffering. Those who "fake happy" come off as naive, shallow, and unfeeling. Some of the happiest people I have ever met, such as the Dalai Lama, have experienced indescribable suffering in their lives, and hence manifest genuineness and empathy in their interactions with others (Dalai Lama & Cutler, 1998).

While being mindful can foster a sense of gratitude and appreciation, and can lead to a feeling of happiness, if you do this as a way of avoiding your problems, it will create more problems in the future, because it leads to endless cycles of struggle with your own emotions. Feelings are meant to flow, not to be fixed.

Taking time to be mindful and appreciative of what we have to be grateful for can be a wonderful thing to add to our daily routines. However, we cannot hold on to any feeling state, including happiness. We will always have responsibilities and practical problems that need to be dealt with. We will handle our problems much more effectively if we pay attention. This is much different than getting lost in ruminations or worries about problems. We can make room for all our emotions, and we can make choices to engage in activities that give us greater fulfillment.

There is a difference between feeling happy and feeling fulfilled. For example, if you are a parent, there are moments of great joy, great sadness, great anger, and great fear. Parents who try to always be happy will not equip their children to deal with the challenges of the modern world. Yet, despite all the challenges, parenting can be very fulfilling, especially if you pay attention and are present as the journey unfolds.

Some people are also pursuing a future happiness. They work hard and sacrifice for an imagined future time when all will be well. While it is important to plan for the future, the only time you can feel anything is in the present moment.

Summary: Mindfulness is about being present in the moment. At times, feelings of happiness will come, but such feelings cannot be forced to come into existence, and they cannot be grasped and held on to. Happiness is more likely to come as a natural "side effect" of living in the present moment. The only time you can feel is in the present. When you stay out of your own way, it is natural to feel pain when you are hurt, sadness when something is lost, anger when an injustice is done, and happiness when you notice what you have to be grateful for.

Further Resources

Dalai Lama, & Cutler, H. C. (1998). *The art of happiness: A handbook for living*. London: Hodder & Stoughton.

Emmons, R. A. (2008). Gratitude, subjective well-being, and the brain. In M. Eid & R. J. Larsen (Eds.), *The science of subjective well-being*, 469–489. Guilford Press.

Emmons, R. A. (2007). *Thanks!: How the new science of gratitude can make you happier.* Houghton Mifflin Harcourt.

Harris, R. (2008). *The happiness trap: How to stop struggling and start living.* Trumpeter.

McCullough, M. E., Tsang, J. A., & Emmons, R. A. (2004). Gratitude in intermediate affective terrain: links of grateful moods to individual differences and daily emotional experience. *Journal of Personality and Social Psychology, 86*(2), 295.

Rāhula, W. (1974). *What the Buddha taught.* Grove Press.

Tirch, D., Silberstein, L. R., & Kolts, R. L. (2015). *Buddhist psychology and cognitive-behavioral therapy: A clinician's guide.* Guilford Publications.

Myth: Mindfulness is about having a clear, empty, or blank mind.

Since human minds are often so full of rambling thoughts, some people believe that the goal of mindfulness is to be able to clear one's mind of all thoughts. In fact, in one study, almost half of those surveyed said they believe that mindfulness is about having an empty mind (Lester, Murrell, & Dickson, 2018).

Basis in truth: Words and thoughts are useful tools that human beings have developed to describe, evaluate, and problem-solve, which has great survival value (Bach & Moran, 2008; Hayes, Strosahl, & Wilson, 2012; Torneke, 2010). I can describe a snake as a long, slithering animal with sharp teeth. I can evaluate it as a threat because I remember that I saw it bite another person. I can then problem-solve by running away from it or climbing up a tree until it goes away.

But this gift of language can also become a curse, becoming a filter through which all reality is distorted. It can create mental realms that do not exist in the real world, which can even create life-threatening problems. If I describe myself as completely unable to keep a job or a relationship, I might evaluate myself as being a loser. I could then problem-solve by taking my own life. We are the only species with symbolic language, and the only species who will intentionally commit suicide.

Mindfulness can help free us from the grip of compulsive thinking, which often interferes with direct perception of reality through the senses. To say, "This sunset is red" does not do justice to the experience.

The richness of color experienced though our eyes cannot possibly be captured in the word "red." There are often moments in mindfulness practice when we are able to step back from thoughts. When the stranglehold of thoughts is loosened, we can be fully present in our senses.

When someone talks all the time, they never hear what anyone else has to say. Likewise, when we think all the time, we have nothing to think about except thoughts (Watts, 1957). There are sometimes moments in mindfulness practice when discursive thoughts are suspended and the mind falls silent, even in the midst of chaos. It feels like all filters fall away, leaving reality clearly and brightly shining through.

There are also certain types of meditation other than mindfulness that create a state of consciousness in which thoughts fall away. Though this experience can happen to anyone at any time, these exercises typically require years of practice, involving intense concentration on an object or sound, as in chanting of hymns or sacred sounds known as mantra (Dalai Lama, Tsong-ka-pa, & Hopkins, 1987; Hayes, 2019).

Reality: Just as the pancreas produces insulin, the thinking centers of the cortex of the brain produce thoughts and images. There are times when the mind settles on its own, just as muddy water when left alone naturally clears. However, trying to calm the mind by force is like trying to calm waves with a flat iron, or like trying to clear the water in a snow globe by shaking it vigorously.

Research even shows that trying to stop thoughts only increases our struggles with them (Wang, Hagger, & Chatzisarantis, 2020; Wegner, Schneider, Carter, & White, 1987). If I tell you that something bad will happen if you think of a pink elephant, you will try not to think of a pink elephant, and your mind will hence be thinking about not thinking about a pink elephant. You can distract yourself temporarily, but such thoughts tend to keep coming back, because the act of fighting them off conditions them with even more emotion.

Thoughts can be conditioned to arise automatically (Hayes, Strosahl, & Wilson, 2012; Torneke, 2010). If I say, "Mary had a little . . . ," you are likely to automatically think "lamb" if you heard that song as a child. If for some reason I told you that lamb was a bad word, or that you were a bad person if you thought the word lamb, you would still think it the next time you heard "Mary had a little . . . "

So, the attempt to stop thinking is already thinking about not thinking. In order to understand how thoughts can be conditioned to arise automatically, it may be helpful to discuss the principle of classical conditioning.

Classical conditioning, also known as Pavlovian or respondent conditioning, involves the pairing of a neutral stimulus with a stimulus that naturally activates a biological response, such that the previously neutral stimulus becomes able to activate the biological response.

Most of you are probably familiar with Ivan Pavlov's experiments with his dogs (Pavlov, 1927). Pavlov was actually studying digestion, which was why he conveniently had surgically implanted saliva collection tubes in the dogs. In fact, it was a confound for his digestion experiments that the dogs were drooling before he even got the food to them. Of course, if you are a pet owner, this does not surprise you at all. You know that when you open the cabinet door where you keep the pet food, the squeaking sound sparks the pet to come running from across the house.

Pavlov had the presence of mind to test this phenomenon out empirically. Food (the UCS, or unconditioned stimulus) naturally produces salivation (the UCR, or unconditioned response). However, if the food is presented at the same time a bell is rung (the CS, or conditioned stimulus), and this is done many times, the sound of the bell alone will trigger the salivation response (which then becomes known as the CR, or conditioned response).

Amazingly, the formerly neutral stimulus of the bell sound can now evoke a physiological reaction just as strongly as if there were actually food there. If dogs could talk, you could ask them, "Why are you drooling? You can't eat a bell, much less the sound of a bell!?" The dogs would likely reply, "I don't know! I can't help it! The drool just keeps coming out of my mouth!"

Brain research, initially done on things like starfish and squid, which have larger neurons than humans, shows that brain rewiring takes place during classical conditioning (Carlson & Birkett, 2021). This becomes very important with clinical issues like anxiety, trauma, and addiction. The person might logically know that the physical reactions they are having do not fit the current situation, but they are unable to talk themselves out of it, because it is coming from the emotional part of their brains where the reaction has been classically conditioned. In fact, it was even discovered that the immune system can become classically conditioned, which sparked the development of the field of psychoneuroimmunology (Ader & Cohen, 1975).

Another important clinical consideration is that almost any stimulus can become classically conditioned if it is present with what originally causes a physical reaction. If a woman was once attacked by a man with a beard, her heart may immediately start pounding with fear when she sees someone else with a beard, even though she logically knows that she has no reason to be afraid. As we know, it is not helpful when someone is told to "just stop it" when the reaction is being caused by a response wired in the brain.

Likewise, thoughts can be conditioned to arise in certain contexts and to be embedded with certain emotions (Hayes, 2005). The word "airplane" may not have much emotion for some people. For me, as a private pilot, it evokes feelings of excitement and adventure. For others, it evokes fear and anxiety. Perhaps most interestingly, if you did not speak English, the word "airplane" would have no conditioned associations or emotions.

Rather than stopping thoughts, in mindfulness practice, one begins to notice the automatic conditioned associations and emotions connected to the thoughts. Over time, these associations and emotions can be loosened from the thoughts. One can still understand and use language, but one is no longer bound up by language.

Just as physiological reactions can be conditioned, they can also be extinguished, or to put it more exactly, they can be inhibited from firing automatically (Carlson & Birkett, 2021; Domjan, 2008). If you approach the dogs in Pavlov's experiment and just keep ringing the bell, over and over and over again, without presenting food, the drool response will start diminishing and will eventually stop. This is a very important component of the clinical technique of exposure therapy, which is used to treat anxiety.

There are a couple of important things to keep in mind about the extinction process. One is called spontaneous recovery (Carlson & Birkett, 2021; Recorla & Heth, 1975). If you go back to the dogs a week later, and just for fun, decide to ring the bell again just to see what might happen, the dogs are likely to drool a little. The saliva probably will not flow as strongly as it did previously, and it may not last very long, but nonetheless, traces of the previous brain connections will still be there.

The other important thing to remember is that previously conditioned responses come back much more quickly the next time they are conditioned (Domjan, 2008; Rescorla & Heth, 1975). If you had to ring a bell while presenting the food 100 times to get that strong saliva response, then you extinguish it, it might only take you 30 times to get that same strong salivation the next time, again indicating that the previous brain pathways are still partially there.

Classical conditioning is like building a roadway in the brain. The first time you build a road, it takes a lot of time to dig up the ground, lay the foundation, and top it with asphalt. If you stop using that roadway, it is likely to start falling apart, and weeds will start growing in the cracks. However, the next time you want to start using that roadway, you will be able to get it operational much more quickly.

These concepts are also very important in clinical work. A person can go to a psychotherapist with a problem like anxiety and get better in a relatively short period of time. Yet, a couple of months later, or a couple of years later, they go back to that therapist with the exact same issue they presented with the first time. One of the reasons this happens is that they are falling back into those old, conditioned brain pathways, into those maladaptive "brain grooves" so to speak, and they quit therapy before they have learned how to prevent falling back into those old grooves.

Because of old conditioning, even in a very experienced mindfulness practitioner, certain thoughts will still spark old feelings and emotions, but the practitioner learns not to get caught up in those old patterns, and the reactions tend to diminish over time.

In mindfulness practice, one does not seek to get rid of thoughts, but to get less hooked by or pulled into thoughts. Thoughts will naturally come and go on their own. One comes to perceive thoughts for what they really are—ephemeral phenomena produced by the brain. For this reason, clouds are often used as an analogy for thoughts. They come and go without leaving tracks in the sky, and the sky is not scarred by the clouds. Sometimes the sky is clear and sometimes the sky is full of clouds, but the sky is big enough to contain all the clouds. One cannot push away clouds, and one cannot hold on to clouds. The attempt to do either will only wear one out. The mind is big enough to make room for thoughts without being scarred by them.

Summary: The human brain gets conditioned by the family and one's culture to produce certain thoughts, and those thoughts are often automatically connected to certain emotional responses. Rather than controlling or getting rid of thoughts, mindfulness practice is about allowing them to come and go without getting pulled into unnecessary drama. There are times when the mind settles and thoughts are much less prominent, but one cannot force an absence of thoughts by thinking. It is natural and often useful to have thoughts, as long as one uses thinking rather than is used by thinking. By making space for the thoughts to come and go, one can place one's attention on the direct experience of reality through one's senses.

Further Resources

Bach, P., & Moran, D. J. (2008). *ACT in practice: Case conceptualization in acceptance and commitment therapy*. Oakland, CA: New Harbinger Publications.

Carlson, N. R., & Birkett, M. A. (2021). *Physiology of Behavior*, 13th edition. Pearson.

Hayes, S. C. (2005). *Get out of your mind and into your life: The new acceptance and commitment therapy*. New Harbinger Publications.

Pavlov, I. P. (1927). *Conditioned reflexes: An investigation of the physiological activity of the cerebral cortex*, Trans. G. V. Anrep. New York: Dover.

Torneke, N. (2010). *Learning RFT: An introduction to relational frame theory and its clinical application*. New Harbinger Publications.

Wang, D., Hagger, M. S., & Chatzisarantis, N. L. (2020). Ironic effects of thought suppression: a meta-analysis. *Perspectives on Psychological Science*, *15*(3), 778–793.

Wegner, D., Schneider, D., Carter, S., & White, T. (1987). Paradoxical effects of thought suppression. *Journal of Personality and Social Psychology, 53*, 5–13.

Myth: Mindfulness is about changing consciousness. Some people think that mindfulness involves a radical change in one's state of consciousness, and that people who practice it are living in a constant mystical state. Since they believe mundane life is stressful and dreary, they long for this "higher" state of consciousness.

Basis in truth: Consciousness is a mysterious thing. After many years of intense research, consciousness is still something that scientists find difficult to define, much less to study empirically, and there is much debate on what it is and how it manifests in the brain (Chalmers, 2018; Crick & Koch, 2003; Hameroff & Penrose, 2017). Even though it is difficult to pin down empirically, human beings have sought to change their state of consciousness for thousands of years through a wide variety of means (D'Aquili & Newberg, 1999). Spiritual seekers in particular have a long tradition of using meditative techniques to create a shift in consciousness. Mindfulness has often been taught as a method of stabilizing attention in preparation for more "advanced" forms of meditation designed to produce changes in consciousness.

Shamanic and other spiritual traditions have used a variety of methods to induce trance states, such as chanting, drumming, and using sacred plants like peyote and mushrooms, and these methods continued to be used in modern times. Drumming circles remain popular among certain groups, and use of hallucinogens and other drugs remains widespread in part for the changes in consciousness they produce. I once had one of my therapy clients tell me that using heroin was "like being hugged by God." As was the case for this client, many people feel overwhelmed by their thoughts and feelings, and seek to escape into a different state of consciousness.

If what you consider to be your "normal" state of consciousness is full of thoughts, ideas, and images, then when you come fully into your senses through the practice of mindfulness, it can feel like you are "waking up" to a new state of consciousness (Kabat-Zinn, 2005; Sears, 2017a).

Reality: Mindfulness practice is about becoming more present in this moment, not changing consciousness to some kind of different state. It is about coming to our senses (Kabat-Zinn, 2005; Watts, 2004b).

A story from an ancient koan book called the *Wu Men Guan* describes the futility of seeking some special state of consciousness outside of this moment (Watts, 1957; Wonji Dharma, 2007a). A Zen master was once asked, "What is the Way?" He responded, "Everyday mind is the Way." The student then asked, "How does one accord with it?" "When you try to accord with it, you push it away," the teacher replied.

When I lead people through mindfulness exercises, or attend retreats, it is always interesting to me that when the exercise is over, people sometimes act as if they were returning from a deep sleep. Instead of paying attention in the present, many people are striving for a different state of consciousness. Some of the confusion may lie in the fact that certain other forms of meditation do in fact alter consciousness, which is backed up by scientific brain scans and brain wave recordings (Goleman & Davidson, 2017; Hirai, 1989; Newberg, d'Aquili, & Rause, 2008).

Absorption and other types of consciousness changing meditation can be quite wonderful to experience, but you cannot live daily life in a different state of consciousness. It would be difficult to impossible to drive a car, do your work, or have meaningful relationships in such a state.

Some people are trying to use mindfulness and other types of meditation as a way to avoid or escape from their problems, their uncomfortable feelings, and their distressing thoughts. When you have been suffering, you hope for some alternate reality, or a different state of mind, somehow different from this one. But where else could you possibly go than the here and now? Wherever you go, there you are (Kabat-Zinn, 2009). You are always in the present moment.

Even as I write this, I do not feel any different now than when I am "formally" practicing mindfulness. There is only this moment—there is no difference between this now and a "mindfulness" now. You do not need a "different" state of consciousness to notice the sounds outside your window, the clouds floating through the sky, or the breeze moving over your skin.

Yet, subjectively, you do have a different experience of daily life when you pay attention.

When you take a look around while you are standing on the surface of the Earth, it appears to be flat. But if you have traveled on jet airplanes, and have seen movies of astronauts orbiting the planet, you realize it is a sphere. If you look at the moon, it appears to be a shiny flat disk. When you realize it is a giant ball of rock, even though the sense impression is the same when you look at it, you perceive it differently (Watts, 1958).

When you practice mindfulness, even though everything around you appears the same as it does for everyone else, you also realize that there is so much more depth to apparently discrete objects, beings, and events. You realize that, in a certain sense, everything is interconnected with the entire universe, yet the entire universe is fully manifest in this moment.

Summary: Mindfulness is about direct perception in the present moment, not necessarily about shifting consciousness. There are different types of meditation that are designed to produce changes in consciousness, but mindfulness is about bringing attention into the here and now. Rather than shifting into some kind of "higher" consciousness, mindfulness is about experiencing a more direct consciousness of the senses, which can only be experienced in this moment.

Further Resources

Chalmers, D. (2018). The meta-problem of consciousness. *Journal of Consciousness Studies, 25*(9–10), 6–61.

Crick, F., & Koch, C. (2003). A framework for consciousness. *Nature Neuroscience, 6*(2), 119–126.

Goleman, D., & Davidson, R. J. (2017). *Altered traits: Science reveals how meditation changes your mind, brain, and body.* Penguin.

Hirai, T. (1989). *Zen meditation and psychotherapy.* New York: Japan Publications.

Kabat-Zinn, J. (2005). *Coming to our senses: Healing ourselves and the world through mindfulness.* Hachette UK.

Newberg, A., d'Aquili, E. G., & Rause, V. (2008). *Why God won't go away: Brain science and the biology of belief.* Ballantine Books.

Sears, R. (2017). *The sense of self: Perspectives from science and Zen Buddhism.* New York: Springer Nature.

Watts, A. (1958). *Nature, man and woman.* Pantheon Books.

Wonji Dharma. (2007). *The barrier that has no gate (Wu Men Guan).* Buddha Dharma University Press.

<u>Myth: When you are mindful, you rise above your emotions.</u> A number of people struggle on a daily basis with their own distressing thoughts and feelings, and they believe that the purpose of mindfulness is to control or rise above their emotions and be at peace at all times (Hitchcock, Martin, Fischer, Marando-Blanck, & Herbert, 2016).

Basis in truth: When practicing mindfulness, we can begin to see how complicated our thinking can make things out to be. Because of our habit of preparing for future disasters, our thoughts can create countless problems that do not even exist in reality. When we are fully present in the moment, there are times when things seem so simple and clear. Especially when alone in nature, with no demands upon you, the jumble of emotions can fall away. Watching a beautiful sunset, gazing at a majestic tree, or listening to the musical sound of the wind does not require intellectual analysis or emotional struggle.

Though the distinction is in reality somewhat artificial, wisdom traditions speak of the difference between the "relative world," or the world of daily life in which we relate to beings and things around us as though we were separate from them, and the "absolute world," in which one can experience the "big picture" of the entire universe operating as a whole, in which all things are interconnected as one process (Hayes, 2019). There are moments when we can step back from our involvement in the relative world and glimpse an absolute perspective. Though it sounds nonsensical from a relative viewpoint, from the absolute viewpoint, one feels at peace knowing that everything is exactly as it should be in this moment.

Reality: We cannot live as human beings in the absolute realm. We live out our lives in the relative world. It is easy to find moments of peacefulness and calm in a holy temple on a mountaintop, but it is not a sustainable way of life. (And having stayed on mountaintop temples in the Himalayas, I can tell you that those moments can wear off when you face the reality of food, clothing, shelter, and interacting with others.) One could choose to become a hermit so as not to be bothered by things like earning a living and being involved in relationships, but for most of us, such things give meaning and fulfillment to our lives.

If you have had a rough life, or have been tossed around by emotions, you might think that it would be wonderful to be able to rise above emotions. But having emotions is part of the richness of being a complete human being. If you had no emotions, you would not care if your children died, and therefore would not take steps to feed them or protect them. In this case, even so-called negative emotions like fear serve a purpose (Dalai Lama & Eckman, 2008; Leahy, Tirch, & Napolitano, 2011; Sears, 2014).

In the classic book *Descartes' Error* (Damasio, 2006), the author points out the flaw in Descartes's famous dictum, "I think, therefore I am," because emotions are essential, even to science. How would you even decide what thoughts to think, or what was important, without emotions?

Pardon me for name-dropping, but I have seen the Dalai Lama himself get angry. There was an urgent need for something to change, and the person he was talking to was not listening. However, after he expressed his anger, he turned to another person who approached him for a meeting and greeted her with kindness and compassion. He did not stew on his anger, or plot revenge; he simply felt it and expressed it as needed, then allowed it to pass through him when it was no longer needed.

Since mindfulness is about paying attention, one actually becomes more aware of emotions, not less. Emotions give us information, motivation, and compassion. We can come to see feelings as important messengers. If you try to ignore a messenger with important information, they tend to get louder in an attempt to deliver their information. Rather than fight our messengers, we can learn to appreciate them, whether or not we like the message they are delivering. When we change our relationship with our emotions, they become less extreme. We do not have to let our emotions run our lives. We can appreciate the great value our emotions have, even when they are echoes of past experiences that no longer apply in the present, and we can more freely choose what actions we want to take toward what really matters to us (Hayes, 2005).

Summary: Mindfulness allows us to become more aware of emotions, which gives us more information about what is important in life. When we are not trying to avoid emotions, we can more fully appreciate the simple, beautiful moments that arise in life. Rather than getting rid of emotions, we see them as valuable messengers, even when we do not like the messages they are delivering. Rather than struggling with them, mindfulness practice teaches us to hold our emotions lightly.

We can then make choices based on our values rather than giving in to unhelpful reactions based on avoiding, fighting, or giving in to strong emotions.

Further Resources

Dalai Lama, & Ekman, P. (2008). *Emotional awareness: Overcoming the obstacles to psychological balance and compassion.* Macmillan.

Damasio, A. R. (2006). *Descartes' error.* Random House.

Hayes, S. C. (2005). *Get out of your mind and into your life: The new acceptance and commitment therapy.* New Harbinger Publications.

Hayes, S. K. (2019). *Action meditation: The Japanese diamond and lotus tradition.* Nine Gates Press.

Hitchcock, P. F., Martin, L. M., Fischer, L., Marando-Blanck, S., & Herbert, J. D. (2016). Popular conceptions of mindfulness: Awareness and emotional control. *Mindfulness, 7*(4), 940–949.

Leahy, R. L., Tirch, D., & Napolitano, L. A. (2011). *Emotion regulation in psychotherapy: A practitioner's guide.* Guilford Press.

Sears, R. (2014). *Mindfulness: Living through challenges and enriching your life in this moment.* London, UK: Wiley-Blackwell.

Myth: Mindfulness requires nonjudgmental acceptance of things.

Because the expression "nonjudgmental awareness" is often associated with the definition of mindfulness (e.g., Kabat-Zinn, 2013) some people believe that they must never judge anything or anyone, and completely accept whatever happens.

Basis in truth: Judgments can become filters between our minds and the direct perception of reality. A judgment is often a comparison with a past or future event, which pulls us out of the present, and these judgments can be habitual and nearly continuous.

Negative self-judgments can of course be the most insidious form of judging. When people question themselves, "What if I screw up?" or "What will people think of me?", they are not as focused on what they are doing in that moment, so they are ironically more likely to mess up. Negative judgments can often become self-fulfilling prophecies.

Interestingly, even positive self-judgments can get in the way of direct experience. I do not play the guitar much anymore, but when I do, I sometimes find myself surprised when I am playing a song fairly well that I have not played in a while. However, the moment I think to myself, "Gee, this sounds great!" is usually when I mess up. I lose my focus, get in my own way, and my fingers forget what to do. When I am judging how I am doing, I am not fully present in the moment.

Mindfulness practice helps us learn to notice and temporarily set aside our judgments, allowing us to be more present in this moment through our senses.

In a certain sense, acceptance is also an important practice in mindfulness (Kabat-Zinn, 2013; Salzberg, 2002). Reality is what it is, whether we accept it or not. Wishing things were different does not change them and only creates wasted frustration.

Reality: The word "nonjudgmentally" has caused a lot of confusion, and some have suggested removing this term altogether from the definition of mindfulness. The mind is actually a "judgment factory" (Hayes, Strosahl, & Wilson, 2012). It is programmed to continuously churn out judgments. While the automaticity of these judgments may diminish with the practice of mindfulness, you would not ever want them to completely stop.

Fostering a nonjudgmental attitude does not mean that we get rid of judgments. Judgments can be very important and useful in our lives. You had to make a judgment as to whether or not you thought this book was going to be worth your money and your time to read (hopefully you feel that was a good judgment so far). Given that most of us have limited time and money, making a judgment on how to spend those resources is important. Judging in the positive sense means we discern what is good or bad for us, pay attention to what might be helpful or harmful to others, and compare how things are now with how we want them to be.

However, judgments get us into trouble when we constantly get hooked by them. In mindfulness practice, nonjudgmentally really means temporarily suspending, or setting aside, our constant, habitual, compulsive tendency to judge, or compare, this moment with some other time or some other place. For example, if while you are reading this book, you are constantly judging and thinking to yourself, "This book is okay, but a book by Jon Kabat-Zinn would be better to read. I wonder if I'm ever going to get anything out of this." While that may very well be an accurate judgment, while you are thinking about that, you are not paying much attention to what you are reading right now. You will end up moving your eyes over these words without retaining anything, and I might just make an interesting point every now and then. Of course, it may be useful to pause sometimes to make a judgment, deciding whether or not it's worth it to continue, but constantly judging keeps you in your own head.

We probably all have at least one friend or relative who is never satisfied. No matter how wonderful the moment or activity they are engaged in, they find something about it to judge or compare with something else. When it is cloudy, they complain that there is no sun. When the sun comes out, they complain that the sun is too bright. There is always something you can judge about each moment, but if you do that constantly, it means that you are never fully in any of your moments.

Of course, we do not want to completely throw out our ability to judge, even in mindfulness practice. There have been times I have been leading mindfulness exercises with a group of people when the fire alarm went off. If the fire alarm goes off while you are practicing, you do *not* want to tell yourself, "I am noticing a shrill, piercing sound right now, but I'm not going to judge that. How curious that my respiration is getting increasingly difficult. Interesting that the temperature of my flesh is increasing exponentially." In such an instance, making and acting on a judgment that this is a bad situation and that I should run out of the room could save my life!

However, far more likely than the fire alarm going off, you might hear people talking and laughing nearby. If you start thinking, "I wish those people would shut up and stop being so happy, I'm trying to work on becoming more compassionate over here!", that might be a judgment you want to set aside.

Amusingly, it is common to get caught up in judgments even during mindfulness practice. When you are feeling your breath, your mind might wander off to what you have to do later. "Oh no," you say to yourself. "I'm not supposed to be thinking about other things. I'm supposed to be feeling my breath." Suddenly, it dawns on you that you just judged yourself. "Oops, I'm not supposed to judge myself!" But then you realize, "Darn it! I just judged my judgment of myself!"

In mindfulness practice, we foster the attitude of just noticing, and letting go of struggling with ourselves, as best we can. We simply notice that our minds have wandered off, and bring our attention back to where we want it to be. We notice when judgments arise, or even judgments about judgments about judgments, and just bring our attention back again to where we want it to be. We do not have to justify anything to ourselves or analyze what just happened. After all, they are our own thoughts and feelings. It is up to us to decide if we want to entertain them or refocus our attention elsewhere.

The real question is, are you using judgments when you choose to, or are the judgments using you? Mindfulness helps us more clearly notice judgments, attend to them if necessary, and set them aside when they interfere with our present moment experiences.

This practice helps us accept reality as it is in the present moment. Accepting how things are right now does not mean that you like things as they are. This acceptance may include anger, frustration, and sadness. However, we can only start from where we are (Chodron, 2001).

If you do not accept where you are now, how can you possibly take steps to get to where you want to go? If you do not accept reality, how can you possibly decide what to do about it in the next moment, and if it is even possible to change it (Brach, 2004; Hayes, 2005; Linehan, 2020)?

Summary: Rather than eliminating judgments, mindfulness can help us develop the ability to temporarily set aside the constant, habitual, compulsive tendency to judge or compare this present moment here and now to some other time and place. This allows us to consciously decide whether or not the judgments that do arise are useful or helpful. Acceptance is about noticing reality as it is, which is a prerequisite for making a choice about if, when, and how to make a conscious response.

Further Resources

Brach, T. (2004). *Radical acceptance: Embracing your life with the heart of a Buddha*. Bantam Books.

Chodron, P. (2001). *Start where you are: A guide to compassionate living*. Shambhala Publications.

Hayes, S. C. (2005). *Get out of your mind and into your life: The new acceptance and commitment therapy*. New Harbinger Publications.

Kabat-Zinn, J. (2013). *Full catastrophe living: Using the wisdom of your body and mind to face stress, pain, and illness (revised edition)*. Delta.

Linehan, M. M. (2020). *Dialectical behavior therapy in clinical practice*. Guilford Publications.

Salzberg, S. (2002). *Lovingkindness: The revolutionary art of happiness*. Shambhala Publications.

Sears, R. (2014). *Mindfulness: Living through challenges and enriching your life in this moment*. London, UK: Wiley-Blackwell.

3 Myths about How Mindfulness Is Similar and Different

The human mind likes to categorize things and make comparisons. If something is new to you, your brain will often attempt to fit that new information into some category you already know. Social psychology has long talked about confirmation bias, or the tendency to look for information that supports your point of view while ignoring contradictory information (Klayman, 1995; Nickerson, 1998; Wason, 1960). If you think people are mean, you will tend to notice acts of rudeness and ignore acts of kindness. If you think people are nice, you will tend to notice acts of kindness and ignore acts of rudeness. If you already think you know what mindfulness is, you will find lots of other people, websites, and books that agree with you, and you will tend to ignore anything that contradicts what you think you know.

At the other extreme, if you do not understand something, your mind will tell you it is completely different from what you already know. In the case of mindfulness, it is often misunderstood because it is so simple and ordinary. The attempt to categorize and describe an everyday sensory experience in words or scientific descriptions creates problems in the mind that do not even exist in the real world.

It is important to recognize how mindfulness is different from other methods. Of course, in emphasizing differences, I do not mean to imply that one technique or method is better than another, or that you should only use mindfulness. Personally, I want as many tools as possible in my toolbox to help equip me to handle the challenges of life. However, it is important to understand each tool and what it is designed for in order to use it most effectively.

This chapter will explore myths about the similarities and differences between mindfulness and breathing exercises, meditation, visualization, relaxation, and hypnosis.

Myth: Mindfulness is just breathing. When some people think of mindfulness, they imagine people are just sitting still and breathing deeply, which sounds terribly boring to them.

Basis in truth: There is an ancient practice, originating in India, called *pranayama* (literally, controlling or regulating the breath or life force; Van Lysebeth, 1979). This practice involves changing your breath on purpose to alter the body's physiological responses. Modern science now understands more clearly how this works. Breathing quickly and shallowly activates the sympathetic nervous system to increase energy and alertness. Breathing deeply and slowly activates the parasympathetic nervous system to increase relaxation (Carlson & Birkett, 2021; Kabat-Zinn, 2013; Sears, 2017b).

A focus on breathing is often something used by people who practice mindfulness (Buddhadasa Bhikkhu, 1996; Kabat-Zinn, 2013; Segal, Williams, & Teasdale, 2013; Teasdale, Williams, & Segal, 2014). Conveniently, if you are alive, you are probably breathing, so it is always available as an object of attention.

Another reason that paying attention to the breath is useful as a mindfulness practice is because the breath can give us a great deal of information about our physical and emotional state. Most children breathe naturally and deeply from the diaphragm, colloquially referred to as "belly breathing." Adults are more likely to be in their heads worrying about the future, and they tend to breathe more shallowly from the chest. Pausing to notice how you are breathing can give you data about your emotional state. Many people do not even realize they are breathing quickly from the chest or even holding their breaths sometimes. Such rapid and shallow breathing is correlated with an active sympathetic nervous system, which is what fires the stress response (Carlson & Brirkett, 2021; Sapolsky, 2004).

Though it is technically a visualization practice and not mindfulness, a common metaphor used in mindfulness practice is "breathing into" difficult experiences. When most people are uncomfortable, they consciously or unconsciously brace themselves against it, tensing up their muscles, raising the stress response, and creating even more suffering. "Breathing into" one's experiences, even into pain and uncomfortable emotions, can be useful for moving directly into experiences as a remedy to counter the tendency to struggle with, avoid, or push away unpleasant experiences. The practice helps one to hold one's difficulties with gentle attention and compassion.

Breathing is both a conscious and an unconscious process, which also makes it a useful tool for learning mindfulness. If you wish, you can notice and control your rate of breathing right now. But your breathing continues whether or not you notice it. The same is true of other things, like thoughts—you can choose to think something, and thoughts also arise by themselves. Some people become anxious when they try to control or not control their breath or their thoughts, and working through this artificially created struggle teaches one to let go of self-created feedback loops of struggle.

Reality: There are a variety of wonderful breath exercises for achieving all types of purposes. While they may seem very similar, mindfulness practices focus on the development of present moment awareness. For example, deep breathing can be a wonderful way to activate the parasympathetic nervous system, which activates the relaxation response (Benson & Klipper, 2009; Kabat-Zinn, 2013; Sapolsky, 2004). However, sometimes deep breathing can become a form of avoidance. If I cannot stand my own emotions, and forcefully breathe deeply to distract myself from them or to make them go away, I am ironically likely to increase my struggle, given that the emotions are mine and not a foreign invader.

Mindfulness is not about adding struggle to difficult situations. It is about noticing first, then making a choice. If I notice unpleasant emotions, and recognize that I am struggling, I can allow the emotions to be exactly as they are (since they are what they are whether I accept them or not in that moment). I can then choose to take some deep breaths as a gesture of self-compassion. The difference between avoidance and self-compassion can seem subtle, but the subjective experiences are vastly different.

Sometimes the breath is used as a focus for concentration exercises. Such exercises often involve counting the breath, thinking about the breath, or creating a mental image of the breathing process in the mind. While these can be useful exercises, in mindfulness practice, we are feeling the breath, directly experiencing it in the present moment, not thinking about it or picturing it in our minds. A great deal of trouble can arise when we confuse reality as experienced through the senses with internally created thoughts and images.

Since mindfulness is just paying attention, the breath is only one thing on which you could choose to place your attention. There is a lot more going on in the present moment besides the breath. There are almost countless experiences to notice in any given moment, both within yourself and all around you, which is why there are almost countless different types of mindfulness practices.

Summary: Many mindfulness exercises make use of the breath for a variety of purposes, such as developing the ability to intentionally keep awareness where one chooses, moving into difficult experiences, distinguishing between sensory perceptions and mental representations, and on exploring the seeming distinction between conscious and unconscious processes. One can be mindful of the breath, but mindfulness is so much more than just noticing the breath, so there are a wide variety of formal mindfulness practices. Ultimately, the point of practice is to become more fully present to the richness of experience in every moment.

Further Resources

Benson, H., & Klipper, M. Z. (2009). *The relaxation response*. New York: Morrow.

Buddhadasa Bhikkhu (1996). *Mindfulness with breathing: A manual for serious beginners*. Wisdom Publications.

Kabat-Zinn, J. (2013). *Full catastrophe living: Using the wisdom of your body and mind to face stress, pain, and illness (revised edition)*. Delta.

Sapolsky, R. M. (2004). *Why zebras don't get ulcers: The acclaimed guide to stress, stress-related diseases, and coping*. Holt paperbacks.

Sears, R. (2017). *The cognitive-behavioral therapy and mindfulness toolbox*. Eau Claire, WI: PESI Publishing & Media, Inc.

Teasdale, J., Williams, M., & Segal, Z. (2014). *The mindful way workbook: An 8-week program to free yourself from depression and emotional distress*. New York: Guilford Press.

Van Lysebeth, A. (1979). *Pranayama: The yoga of breathing*. Unwin Paperbacks.

Myth: Mindfulness is the same as meditation. People often use the terms mindfulness and meditation interchangeably, and believe they are the same thing.

Basis in truth: If we define meditation as a method of working with the mind, then mindfulness is definitely a type of meditation, especially when practiced in a formal, structured way. When first learning mindfulness, many teachers suggest structured mindfulness practices as the best way to exercise and develop one's attentional capacity (Kabat-Zinn, 2013; Segal, Williams, & Teasdale, 2013).

In many meditative traditions, mindfulness is considered a foundational or preparatory practice. It is hard to do sophisticated forms of meditation if one cannot keep one's mind focused and present (Hopkins, 1992; Luk, 1964; McDonald, 2005; Thrangu, 1993).

Reality: Mindfulness can be done as formal meditation practices, as for example, when one sits on a cushion and sets a timer while paying attention to the body or the breath. However, one can be mindful without doing meditation (Harris, 2009). One can also be mindful in any moment: when driving a car, talking to a friend, or opening your mail (Kabat-Zinn, 2005; Sears, 2014; Segal, Williams, & Teasdale, 2013).

There are literally thousands of different kinds of meditation, and they differ in important ways from mindfulness practice. One can meditate on a specific subject, like interdependence, impermanence, death, and the nature of self, in order to work through fears and misunderstandings of such things (Hopkins, 1992; Sears, Tirch, & Denton, 2011; Sears, 2017). One can practice absorption type meditations in order to experience a shift in consciousness in which the perceived boundaries and limitations of the self, which are created by thinking, expand and dissolve, seemingly into the entire universe (McDonald, 2005; Sears, 2017a; Wallace, 1970). Chanting, or repeating specific symbolic or meaningful sounds called mantra, can also produce shifts in consciousness, can help focus the mind, or can reprogram one's thinking and perception (Dalai Lama, Tsong-ka-pa, & Hopkins, 1987; Hayes, 2019; Khalsa, Amen, Hanks, Money, & Newberg, 2009). Some types of meditation are intended to create changes in the way one thinks and feels, such as through systematically fostering the capacity to embody loving-kindness (Hofmann, Grossman, & Hinton, 2011; Salzberg, 2002). One can also practice visualization exercises, in which one creates a specific internal or external experience through imagery in order to change one's experience of oneself and/or the external world. Some forms of meditation are designed to create a more conscious, integrated self, often by visualizing inspirational, archetypal forms that represent what one wants to become (Luk, 1964; McDonald, 2005).

While these and other types of meditation can have useful and even amazing effects, both subjectively and scientifically, their design and purpose differ from the practice of mindfulness. In contrast to the above forms of meditation, mindfulness is simply paying attention to how things are in this moment. In fact, in certain traditions, all these "higher" meditation practices simply lead one back to the richness of the present moment, coming full circle, as there is nowhere else to be but here and now.

Summary: All types of meditation are not mindfulness, though mindfulness can be a type of meditation. While it can often serve as an important prerequisite to other forms of meditation that require the ability to stay focused, mindfulness is simply paying attention in the present moment and is not necessarily about changing consciousness, visualizing, or chanting.

Further Resources

Dalai Lama, Tsong-ka-pa, & Hopkins, J. (1987). *Tantra in Tibet: The great exposition of secret mantra*, Vol. 1. Snow Lion Publications.

Harris, R. (2009). Mindfulness without meditation. *Healthcare Counselling and Psychotherapy Journal, 9*(4), 21–24.

Hayes, S. K. (2019). *Action meditation: The Japanese diamond and lotus tradition*. Nine Gates Press.

Hopkins, J. (1992). *Walking through walls: A presentation of Tibetan meditation*. Snow Lion Publications.

Luk, C. (1964). *The secrets of Chinese meditation*. Samuel Weiser.

McDonald, K. (2005). *How to meditate: A practical guide*. Simon and Schuster.

Salzberg, S. (2002). *Lovingkindness: The revolutionary art of happiness*. Shambhala Publications.

Thrangu, K. (1993). *The practice of tranquility and insight: A guide to Tibetan Buddhist meditation*. Boston, MA: Shambhala Publications.

<u>Myth: Mindfulness is about visualizing peaceful scenes and positive outcomes.</u> Some people believe that mindfulness is about creating internal worlds of peace and images of a positive future. Because they see the real world as full of chaos and hopelessness, they hope to change this through imagining a better world.

Basis in truth: There are certain types of meditation that emphasize visualization. In the Buddhist Vajrayana traditions, for example, the practitioner visualizes images that represent the qualities that one wishes to embody, and mentally creates a more enlightened world (Batchelor, 1987; Hayes, 2019). In more mundane terms, in order to have a positive outcome for one's goals, it helps if one can clearly have in mind what that outcome will look like.

Since mindfulness is about developing the ability to pay attention in the moment, such stability of attention can be an important prerequisite to clearly visualizing one's desired goals.

Reality: As discussed in the previous myth, this myth results from a confusion of mindfulness with other types of meditation. While mindfulness is a type of meditation, it is technically noticing reality in the present moment, not creating internal visualizations (Siegel, Germer, & Olendzki, 2009; Sears, 2014). To create a picture in one's mind is to insert a filter between reality and direct experience. While pictures can be appreciated for their beauty, they are only representations of reality. Mindfulness practice is like scraping a painting off of a window to see the actual beauty of nature outside the window.

Popular beliefs about visualizations have contributed to the perpetuation of this myth. In her book *The Secret* (Byrne, 2008), the author basically posits that clearly visualizing something is the secret to manifesting it in the universe. While important, the Buddhist Vajrayana tradition, as well as secular project managers, notes that there are at least two more essential pieces to manifesting something in the world: having and communicating a plan and taking physical action steps. Together, these three pieces become a powerful way to achieve goals (Das, 1998; Hayes, 2019).

There is a sad side effect to believing that visualizing something makes it come true. I have worked with people who accidentally thought something negative, like a family member dying, and then developed severe anxiety that they were going to make it happen. Trying not to think about something means you are thinking about not thinking about it, and you can get caught in a terrible vicious circle. It is the nature of the mind to produce random thoughts, which at its best results in creativity. It is also difficult if not impossible to not think about something on purpose. If I tell you not to think about a purple tree, you are already thinking about what you do not want to think about. Adding anxiety to the thought or image only increases its salience, making it harder to forget.

Choosing to visualize a peaceful scene or positive outcome can be relaxing or inspiring, and can contribute to overall self-care by taking a break from the demands of work and family. However, sometimes these methods are used to compulsively avoid dealing with an unpleasant reality in the moment. If one is using visualization methods to avoid feeling unpleasant feelings or to try not to think distressing thoughts, one may end up inadvertently setting up a vicious cycle of struggle that only increases stress in the long run.

Mindfulness itself is just paying attention. It is up to the individual what to do with that attention. Of course, one can mindfully choose to visualize a peaceful scene or a positive outcome. If one acknowledges reality for what it is, then chooses to visualize a peaceful scene, one is less likely to get caught in avoidance cycles. If one gets in touch with one's values, then practices clearly visualizing a positive outcome, it can help motivate and inspire one to move toward those goals and values, keeping in mind that steps can only be taken in the present moment.

Summary: In many traditions, mindfulness was used as a first step before being ready to have the attentional capacity to practice mediations that involved complex visualizations. While visualization can sometimes be useful, and can be done mindfully, mindfulness practice is about noticing reality as it is in the present moment. Practicing mindfulness helps us discern the difference between internal representations and physical reality, allowing us to make more conscious and wiser choices.

Further Resources

Batchelor, S. (1987). *The jewel in the lotus: A guide to the Buddhist traditions of Tibet.* Wisdom Publications.

Das, L. S. (1998). *Awakening the Buddha within: Eight steps to enlightenment: Tibetan wisdom for the western world.* Harmony.

Hayes, S. K. (2019). *Action meditation: The Japanese diamond and lotus tradition.* Nine Gates Press.

Sears, R. (2014). *Mindfulness: Living through challenges and enriching your life in this moment.* London, UK: Wiley-Blackwell.

Siegel, R. D., Germer, C. K., & Olendzki, A. (2009). Mindfulness: What is it? where did it come from?. In: F. Didonna (Ed.), *Clinical handbook of mindfulness.* New York: Springer. https://doi.org/10.1007/978-0-387-0 9593-6_2

Myth: Mindfulness is the same as relaxation. Many people practice mindfulness in order to relax, and if they do not relax, they believe they are doing it wrong. In fact, in one study, 96% of those surveyed said they believe mindfulness is about relaxation (Lester, Murrell, & Dickson, 2018).

Basis in truth: When I lead people through mindfulness exercises, they often notice that they have muscle tension in their bodies, as if they have been keeping themselves on guard, bracing for something dangerous to happen. When you pause to check in with yourself, and give attention to your own thoughts, feelings, and body sensations, you may realize that you have been holding tension in your body. Once you recognize that you are holding tension that is not needed in this moment, you may choose to let it go, and therefore have the experience of relaxing when practicing mindfulness.

Likewise, when you disengage from your frantic daily activities and pay attention to your internal experiences, you might notice your mind swirling with thoughts and emotions. When you remember that these thoughts and feelings are your own, and not outside invaders, it is like realizing that you have been having a tug of war with your own two hands. Rather than pull harder, you can choose to let go of the struggle with yourself. When you no longer feed the struggle, you often experience a calming of the mind and body.

Reality: There are similarities as well as significant differences between mindfulness and relaxation (Luberto, Hall, Park, Haramati, & Cotton, 2020). While both are important, and both can lead to a relaxed state, they have different theoretical foundations and involve different intentions.

Relaxation methods are intentionally designed to reduce external stimulation and activate the parasympathetic nervous system. This can be accomplished in a wide variety of ways. Visualization exercises involve imagining yourself to be in peaceful, relaxing surroundings, like at the beach or in a pleasant country meadow. Deep breathing alters the balance of oxygen and carbon dioxide to trigger the relaxation response (Benson & Klipper, 2009). Progressive muscle relaxation helps clients distinguish between tension and relaxation by systematically tensing and releasing muscle groups throughout the body (Jacobson, 1938; McKay & Fanning, 2008). You can also simply engage in a relaxing activity, like watching a movie, reading a book, or sitting in a hot tub.

Relaxation methods are akin to taking mini vacations. Taking regular vacations can be an important way to get a break from the stress of life in order to recharge and rejuvenate. In general, a lot of people in our busy modern society could use more vacations and more relaxation.

However, many people are so programmed to "be productive" they have difficulty letting go and letting themselves relax. Even on vacation, they may constantly find themselves checking their cell phones. Even if they manage to relax and enjoy themselves, they grow worried as the end of the vacation approaches. They start to feel "normal" again while on vacation, but then are thrust back into the stress and chaos of work and daily life when they return. All the work they were already behind on gets piled up with all the work they were not doing on vacation, so they may even regret going. Any health and wellness benefits they gain on vacation tend to disappear about a week after returning to work (De Bloom, Geurts, & Kompier, 2013; De Bloom, Kompier, Geurts, De Weerth, Taris, & Sonnentag, 2008).

While it is important to take vacations, one also needs to be able to function in a sustainable way in daily life. While relaxation techniques are very useful, it is also important to find a way to be present in the moment, wisely dealing with each life issue as it arises.

Interestingly, I have found that mindfulness can sometimes lead to relaxation more effectively than when you are trying to force relaxation to happen. The title of an old book by the founder of progressive muscle relaxation was called *You Must Relax* (Jacobson, 1934). While the author's intention was undoubtedly to let people know that too much stress is detrimental to one's health and that it is very important to relax, trying to force relaxation has a paradoxical effect. Relaxing involves getting out of one's own way. Trying to force a natural process, like relaxation, can sometimes create a vicious cycle, because when you are not relaxing, your stress rises, which makes you more tense, which increases stress, which increases tension.

Another problem arises when relaxation methods foster unhealthy avoidance. If you cannot stand having a distressing thought, an unpleasant emotion, or an uncomfortable sensation, you might want to close your eyes and visualize something relaxing. While this can sometimes be useful to provide temporary relief, using relaxation methods solely as a way to avoid or distract oneself from unpleasant thoughts, feelings, and sensations often leads to an exacerbation of the symptoms of stress and anxiety. When you open your eyes, all the things you have to deal with will still be waiting for you.

Relaxation works best as a long-term strategy for reducing overall life stress. Since the human body was not meant to constantly fire the stress response, it is important to activate the relaxation response on a regular basis.

However, we cannot live very effectively in modern society in a constant state of relaxation, so we also need the ability to be present with reality as it is. Mindfulness is about embracing the full richness of life, which Jon Kabat-Zinn (2013) calls "full catastrophe living." When you love, you love deeply. When you are hurt, you feel the pain. When someone you care about is suffering, your heart goes out to them. When problems arise, you rise up to the challenge as best you can. This state has also been called "flow" (Csikszentmihalyi, 1990; Engeser, Schiepe-Tiska, & Peifer, 2021).

If I am dodging traffic, I need to be fully present and engaged. When you first learn to drive, you grip the wheel too tightly, are a bit over-vigilant, and worry about what might happen. After you gain experience, you let go of this unnecessary tension. When you are a mindful driver, you are not completely relaxed, but you are not distracted with extraneous worries, anxieties, and tension. You deal with each moment as it comes.

Likewise, when you are present in your life, you learn to let go of unconscious bracing against imagined catastrophes, and you learn to flow with the joys and challenges as they come. You prepare for the future when you can, and learn from the past, but not at the expense of being present in the moment.

Mindfulness fosters increased awareness of present moment sensory experiences, moving more directly even into difficult challenges. Staying present allows one to notice and let go of unnecessary struggles with thoughts, emotions, and body sensations. When you pay attention, you may in fact realize that you are feeling worse than you thought you were. You may notice more thoughts, more emotions, and more muscle tension that you were completely unaware of, and therefore you may feel "worse." But the only way to effectively deal with anything is to be aware of it first, exactly as it is.

When relaxation comes, it is wonderful. When challenges come, we practice staying out of our own way.

Summary: While mindfulness may often lead to relaxation, it is not the goal. We could say that relaxation is often a pleasant "side effect" of mindfulness practice. The intention of mindfulness practice is to notice things as they are in this moment, whether it is pleasant or not. As we become more aware, we may not always like what we find, but it is essential to be aware of reality if we are to engage with it effectively.

Further Resources

Benson, H., & Klipper, M. Z. (2009). *The relaxation response*. New York: Morrow.

Csikszentmihalyi, M. (1990). *Flow: The psychology of optimal experience*. New York: Harper & Row.

De Bloom, J., Geurts, S. A., & Kompier, M. A. (2013). Vacation (after-) effects on employee health and well-being, and the role of vacation activities, experiences and sleep. *Journal of Happiness Studies, 14*(2), 613–633.

Kabat-Zinn, J. (2013). *Full catastrophe living: Using the wisdom of your body and mind to face stress, pain, and illness (revised edition)*. Delta.

Luberto, C. M., Hall, D. L., Park, E. R., Haramati, A., & Cotton, S. (2020). A perspective on the similarities and differences between mindfulness and relaxation. *Global Advances in Health and Medicine, 9*, 2164956120905597.

McKay, M., & Fanning, P. (2008). *Progressive relaxation and breathing: Relaxation & stress reduction audio series* [Audio CD]. New Harbinger.

Myth: Mindfulness is a kind of self-hypnosis. Some people believe that mindfulness is a type of hypnosis, or trance-like state, that one puts oneself into by using suggestion and other techniques.

Basis in truth: Hypnosis is a method of shifting consciousness into a trance state using induction techniques (Gafner & Benson, 2003; Wester & Smith, 1984). In a trance state, the mind is open to retrieve memories or to plant suggestions to reprogram one's thinking (Yapko, 2011). Hypnosis can also be helpful in retrieving memories which have become unavailable to the conscious mind. The hypnotist may also plant suggestions in the subconscious mind to alter how the client thinks and feels, in order to increase confidence, self-esteem, and other qualities, or to reduce maladaptive behaviors like smoking or overeating.

For example, a hypnotist might put someone into a hypnotic state, then make the suggestion that the patient is confident and at peace. The hypnotist plants those thoughts in the subconscious mind to override previous conditioning. Suggestion is a powerful thing, and certain individuals are more suggestible than others (Kirsch & Braffman, 2001).

When a therapist is guiding a patient with a mindfulness exercise, or when someone is listening to a recording of a guided mindfulness practice, there may be some elements of suggestion at play when the person is asked to be fully present, to notice thoughts, feelings, and body sensations without reacting, and to pay attention to the present moment while allowing their experience to be exactly what it is.

Reality: While there may be some overlap between hypnosis and mindfulness, the intention and purpose of each method is different. In hypnosis, the therapist systematically helps the patient move into a different state of consciousness, suspending the analytical mind by such techniques as imagining that one is walking down a deep staircase. Once in the hypnotic state, the intention is to retrieve information or reprogram deeper levels of the mind. This is often done through visualizations of other times and places, or even imagining that one is a different self.

In contrast, the intention in mindfulness practice is to be more fully awake, alert, and present in this moment. Mindfulness is a practice for strengthening conscious attention rather than subduing it. Sometimes the words used in mindfulness exercises are reminiscent of suggestion, but the intention is not necessarily to change the client's thoughts or feelings. Rather, it is to model an attitude of investigating and moving into present moment experiences. While hypnosis creates internal realities through vividly imagining sensory experiences, mindfulness is about noticing one's senses in the present moment (Kabat-Zinn 2005, Lush & Dienes, 2019; Sears, 2014).

Summary: Hypnosis is an intervention that uses induction techniques to subdue the conscious mind in order to communicate with the subconscious mind. Hypnosis is a very useful technique, with plenty of scientific support, and there is some overlap with mindfulness in how it is used. However, the intent in hypnosis is to shift consciousness to work with the subconscious mind, whereas mindfulness is about being more conscious, alert, and attentive in the present moment.

Further Resources

Gafner, G., & Benson, S. (2003). *Hypnotic techniques: For standard psychotherapy and formal hypnosis.* WW Norton & Co.

Kabat-Zinn, J. (2005). *Coming to our senses: Healing ourselves and the world through mindfulness.* Hachette UK.

Lush, P., & Dienes, Z. (2019). Time perception and the experience of agency in meditation and hypnosis. *PsyCh Journal, 8*(1), 36–50.

Sears, R. (2014). *Mindfulness: Living through challenges and enriching your life in this moment.* London, UK: Wiley-Blackwell.

Yapko, M. D. (2011). *Mindfulness and hypnosis: The power of suggestion to transform experience.* WW Norton & Company.

Wester, W. C., & Smith, A. H. (1984). *Clinical hypnosis: A multidisciplinary approach.* Lippincott Williams & Wilkins.

4   Myths about the Practice of Mindfulness

There are many ideas about how mindfulness is supposed to be practiced. Evidence-based psychotherapy programs like Mindfulness-Based Stress Reduction (Kabat-Zinn, 2013), Mindfulness-Based Cognitive Therapy (MBCT) (Segal, Williams, & Teasdale, 2013), and Dialectical Behavior Therapy (Linehan, 2020) use clear protocol manuals with specific ways of practicing mindfulness. This is necessary in order to consistently replicate these programs to test their effectiveness. Similarly, historical meditation manuals often give specific instructions so that beginners do not have to reinvent the wheel. Unfortunately, these historical and modern programs can give people the impression that what they recommend are rigid rules rather than helpful guidelines.

These modern and historical practice guidelines may give people the impression that they are not cut out to practice mindfulness, that they must practice mindfulness through formal exercises on a daily basis, that practice takes a great deal of effort, that it must be done sitting still and with eyes closed, that it must be done for an uncomfortably long period of time, and that they must move slowly to be mindful. Sadly, these misconceptions may prevent some individuals from ever even trying a mindfulness exercise. In this chapter, we will explore myths about how mindfulness is practiced.

<u>Myth: Only great saints can do mindfulness—it's not for me.</u>
Because they find it very difficult to pay attention, some people think

it would take superhuman abilities to practice mindfulness, therefore they do not even attempt to do it.

Basis in truth: In our educational system, with some notable exceptions, we are taught to live in our heads. We are programmed to plan for and live for the future. We juggle hundreds of concerns in our minds in the hopes that doing so will make life better. Hence, people often have trouble paying attention. Even when things are fairly okay, our minds begin to wander out of habit. Therefore, to many people mindfulness can sound either impossibly challenging or incredibly dull.

Some people do not think they are cut out to do mindfulness because they often fall asleep when they first begin practicing. For many people, the only time they ever stop moving and stop thinking and worrying is when it is time to sleep, so they are conditioned to drift off automatically. Another common reason this happens is due to sleep deprivation. According to a study by the American Psychological Association (2014), adults get an average of 6.7 hours of sleep per night, despite the fact that 7–9 hours is the minimum recommendation (National Sleep Foundation, 2021). There always seems to be more things to get done at the end of the day and some reason to wake up early. Over time, we accumulate quite a bit of sleep debt, which significantly impairs our cognitive and attentional capacities.

It is important to note that sleep has a big impact on attention, which is why lack of it can make mindfulness practice very challenging. Sleep issues are often missed by health care professionals. All of us get cranky or irritable or goofy when we are sleep deprived. Sleep disorders, such as apnea, hypopnea, and restless leg syndrome can create problems that appear to manifest as mental health disorders. Many mental health disorders also significantly affect sleep.

These challenges, whether due to sleep deprivation or mind wandering, can lead some people to think that it would be impossible for them to be mindful.

Reality: Everyone has challenges when first learning mindfulness. Paying attention to and working through obstacles is part of the process of learning.

Making regular sleep a priority can have significant effects on attention and mental health. Amazingly, studies of children with Attention-Deficit/Hyperactivity Disorder (ADHD) have shown that when the only intervention is sleep hygiene—making sure they get enough quality sleep every night—ADHD symptoms improve significantly (Moreau, Rouleau, & Morin, 2013).

Psychoeducation about sleep, or interventions such as cognitive-behavioral therapy for insomnia, can make a world of difference for some people (Perlis, Jungquist, Smith, & Posner, 2008). Interestingly, recent research suggests that the temperature of the room may be even more important for good sleep than consistently going to bed at the same time (Reddy, 2016). The research found that turning the thermostat down to around 65 degrees Fahrenheit resulted in better, deeper sleep. This makes logical sense, since our brains have evolved to go to sleep at night, when the temperature naturally gets cooler. This is also probably why taking a hot bath right before bedtime can help you fall asleep—as your body temperature drops after getting out of the bathtub, your brain believes it is time for sleep.

When one gets better sleep, mindfulness becomes easier to practice. It can also be helpful to practice sitting up instead of lying down, and to experiment with leaving the eyes slightly open instead of fully closed.

Mind wandering is a fairly common issue for most people. In itself, mind wandering is not a bad thing—it contributes to creativity. Though it can seem challenging at first, our attentional capacity can be consciously exercised through mindfulness practice (Giannandrea, Simione, Pescatori, Ferrell, Belardinelli, Hickman, & Raffone, 2019). Each time you notice the mind wandering, and bring it back to where you want it to be, you are exercising the attentional channels of the brain. This principle is known as "Hebb's Rule," which can be summarized as "neurons that fire together, wire together" (Hebb, 1949; Siegel, 2007).

To take a step back and get a broader perspective, it is ridiculous to say someone cannot be mindful. If you think you cannot be in the present moment, where else could you be? Even when you are thinking about the past and the future, you are doing it now. If you tell me that your mind is always thinking about other things, you noticed that in that moment, and hence you were mindful.

Of course, I never tell people they have to practice mindfulness. I simply tell people that anyone who wants to practice can find some benefits.

Summary: It is common for people to face a number of obstacles or challenges when they begin practicing mindfulness, like compulsive mind wandering or falling asleep. However, every human being can become more aware of present moment experience. If you tell me you cannot be mindful, even saying so indicates that you are aware that your mind does not stay for long where you want it to be, and hence you are mindful of that. Regular practice simply strengthens one's attentional capacity.

Further Resources

Giannandrea, A., Simione, L., Pescatori, B., Ferrell, K., Belardinelli, M. O., Hickman, S. D., & Raffone, A. (2019). Effects of the mindfulness-based stress reduction program on mind wandering and dispositional mindfulness facets. *Mindfulness*, *10*(1), 185–195.

National Sleep Foundation. (2021). How much sleep do we really need? Retrieved from http://www.sleepfoundation.org/article/how-sleep-works/how-much-sleep-do-we-really-need

Perlis, M. L, Jungquist, C., Smith, M. T., & Posner, D. (2008). *Cognitive behavioral treatment of insomnia: A session by session guide*. Springer.

Reddy, S. (2016). The best temperature for a good night's sleep: Light and time aren't as important as temperature, new research shows. *Wall Street Journal*, February 22.

Siegel, D. J. (2007). *The mindful brain: Reflection and attunement in the cultivation of well-being* (Norton series on interpersonal neurobiology). WW Norton & Company.

Myth: <u>Mindfulness can only be done with formal, daily exercises.</u>
Some believe that the practice of mindfulness requires specific formal, structured exercises every day, and if you are not doing that, you are not really practicing mindfulness.

Basis in truth: If you want to get into shape, it is not enough to watch a video or to take a class. Regular physical activity is required to maintain optimal physical health. To gain physical health in the most efficient way, a structured, routine approach with gradually increasing intensity is ideal.

Likewise, if you want to develop your attentional capacity in the most efficient way, it can be helpful to have a routine, structured, graduated approach of formal exercises that have been tested and used for centuries. You might begin with paying attention to an engaging activity like eating a raisin. You might then practice systematically noticing internal body sensations, as in the body scan. You could then practice feeling the breath, noticing the entire body all at once, and mindfully listening to sounds. You could practice mindfulness in motion, as in mindful walking or mindful stretching. As your skills increased, you could practice a mindfulness of thoughts exercise. You would then be ready to practice mindfully working with difficult or challenging experiences and would be able to integrate mindfulness more naturally into your daily life.

After decades of research, this gradual and systematic approach to training people in mindfulness has worked well in MBSR (Kabat-Zinn, 2013), MBCT (Segal, Williams, & Teasdale 2013), and other programs, so it has continued to be promoted. Those who learned mindfulness from meditative traditions take comfort in using formal exercises that have worked for thousands of years.

Reality: There is some debate among psychology experts about the importance of daily, formal mindfulness exercises. Proponents of eight-week training programs like MBSR and MBCT tend to emphasize the importance of daily, structured practice. Other approaches, like ACT, place primary emphasis on bringing mindfulness into daily life and are less likely to ask people to practice formal daily exercises. They often employ "mindfulness without meditation" (Harris, 2009) because many people are reluctant or unwilling to do formal practices for a variety of reasons, but they still find ways to help people benefit from increased present moment awareness.

The research has produced mixed results in terms of whether or not formal, daily mindfulness exercises are essential to improve one's mental health or quality of life (Epstein, 2017; Wimmer, Bellingrath, & von Stockhausen, 2020). While meta-analyses have shown an overall small association with reported mindfulness practice and positive outcomes, these results are not universal (Lloyd, White, Eames, & Crane, 2018; Parsons, Crane, Parsons, Fjorback, & Kuyken, 2017). In fact, some research shows no correlation, and some shows that increased mindfulness is correlated with decreased homework practice (Byerly-Lamm, 2017; Ribeiro, Atchley, & Oken, 2018).

It seems likely that the bottom line is that there is no one best approach for all individuals. Some may benefit from structured practices, others may not. However, a few analogies may be helpful in choosing the path best for you, as the dilemma between structured daily practice and flexible freedom is common across a variety of disciplines.

Physical exercise provides a good analogy. If I go to the gym and engage in a formal workout routine every day, it will be a good way to help ensure I am consistently maintaining my physical health. However, someone else might argue that they do not need to go to the gym, but that they can incorporate exercise into their daily lives. They regularly park their cars farther away in parking lots and get exercise from walking. They take the stairs instead of the elevator. They chop wood for their fireplaces. They play basketball with their kids.

A good argument can be made for either approach. Most would agree though, that if you are currently not in shape, it might be best to set up a structured approach to get a good start.

The problem for some people is that when it rains, they park their cars closer. If they are with friends, they do not want to seem weird by being the only one who takes the stairs. Buying precut firewood is easier. When it gets cold, they stop playing basketball.

Routine appears to be key. Going to the gym can become a habit. However, it can also become a habit to walk, stretch, and do push-ups and sit-ups.

Just as being sedentary can be a habit, getting lost in our minds can also be a habit. Formal mindfulness exercises can be a structured way to break that habit. Being more present and in the senses throughout your day can also become a habit.

Even if you have had the discipline to practice daily formal mindfulness exercises, there comes a time when you can let them go, when "practice" and "daily life" are interwoven. If you are a master guitar player, I can hand you a guitar and ask you to play anything, and it will sound great. If you have never played a guitar before, and I ask you to play anything, it will sound terrible. It takes a certain amount of structured practice and discipline to be able to have complete freedom. You start learning scales and chords when you play guitar, but the point is not to play scales and chords, it is to be free to express yourself in a unique and personal way.

Interestingly, there is even debate among practitioners of ancient meditative traditions. Some schools emphasize that it is essential to do formal practice on a regular basis. Other traditions warn that while it can be important for beginners, it can start to become something artificial and unrelated to daily life.

When I was training to be a Zen teacher, I would interview students with my Zen teacher Wonji Dharma observing me. A student once asked, "I am feeling inspired now, and have been practicing regularly for several years, but I have this fear in the back of my mind that after I leave this retreat, I will slack off and not keep up the practice. How do I avoid slacking off?"

My teacher eyed him carefully. "So, you are making your practice separate. What is correct practice?"

The student thought for a moment, then hesitatingly said, "moment to moment . . ."

My teacher leaned closer to him. "How you keep your mind moment to moment. How can you slack off from your life? So, when you sit on your cushion, you are saying, 'This is my practice, and this is my life.' And you are saying that slacking off can't also be practice."

The silence in the room was palpable, effectively cutting off our thinking. "Why can't you keep moment-to-moment mind while slacking off? What's preventing you from doing that?"

The student smiled. "Absolutely nothing!" A moment of clarity burst through, and we all laughed out loud (Sears, 2014).

I have met many people who have been practicing daily, formal mindfulness practices for decades. This is very commendable. However, some of these people have never learned to bridge what they are practicing into daily life. A regular formal practice can be very helpful for building our ability to pay attention in the moment. But what is the point of only being "present" when you are engaged in formal practice? Why make practice different from daily life? The present moment is the only thing you can experience. What do you see, hear, feel, taste, and smell right now?

It has been said that a practice like mindfulness is a medicine, not a diet (Broughton & Watanabe, 2017; Watts, 2004b). You do not have to keep taking medicine once you have recovered from your illness. However, when the world continuously throws unhealthy things at you, you might choose to take medicine regularly.

Summary: The research has produced mixed results about how essential daily, formal exercises are in order to benefit from mindfulness. Like physical exercise, a regular routine is likely the most efficient way to develop skill, but some people are able to incorporate informal mindfulness practices into their daily life. Just as with physical exercise, it is likely that there is no one formula best for all individuals. In any case, one could say the goal is to be more present in each moment, and one must be cautious not to make formal practice different from one's daily life.

Further Resources

Broughton, J. L., & Watanabe, E. Y. (2017). *The letters of Chan Master Dahui Pujue*. Oxford University Press.

Epstein, D. E. (2017). The role of home practice engagement in a mindfulness-based intervention [ProQuest Information & Learning]. In *Dissertation Abstracts International: Section B: The Sciences and Engineering* (Vol. 77, Issue 9–B(E)).

Harris, R. (2009). Mindfulness without meditation. *Healthcare Counselling and Psychotherapy Journal, 9*(4), 21–24.

Lloyd, A., White, R., Eames, C., & Crane, R. (2018). The utility of home-practice in mindfulness-based group interventions: A systematic review. *Mindfulness, 9*(3), 673–692.

Parsons, C. E., Crane, C., Parsons, L. J., Fjorback, L. O., & Kuyken, W. (2017). Home practice in mindfulness-based cognitive therapy and mindfulness-based stress reduction: a systematic review and meta-analysis of participants' mindfulness practice and its association with outcomes. *Behaviour Research and Therapy, 95*, 29–41.

Ribeiro, L., Atchley, R. M., & Oken, B. S. (2018). Adherence to practice of mindfulness in novice meditators: practices chosen, amount of time practiced, and long-term effects following a mindfulness-based intervention. *Mindfulness, 9*(2), 401–411.

Sears, R. (2014). *Mindfulness: Living through challenges and enriching your life in this moment*. London, UK: Wiley-Blackwell.

Watts, A. (2004b). *Out of your mind: Essential listening from the Alan Watts audio archives* [audio CD]. Boulder, CO: Sounds True.

Wimmer, L., Bellingrath, S., & von Stockhausen, L. (2020). Mindfulness training for improving attention regulation in university students: Is it effective? And do yoga and homework matter?. *Frontiers in Psychology, 11*, 719.

Myth: Mindfulness takes a great deal of effort. One of the reasons some people do not even try to learn mindfulness is because it sounds like a lot of work to do it, and they already feel too overwhelmed with their other responsibilities.

Basis in truth: Most people are raised with exhortations to try hard to get things done. If something is not working, perhaps more effort will pay off. If it is still not working, dig in and keep trying. Therefore, people often approach mindfulness with this same spirit. Because it sounds like it could be difficult, they try hard to pay attention.

Many modern cultures raise their children to become intellectuals. We are taught all kinds of facts in school, and memorization and mental manipulation are emphasized, and that same "trying hard" attitude is encouraged. As Alan Watts (1957) observed, when we are children sitting in a classroom letting our minds wander, teachers often tell us to "Pay attention!" Many children then do their best to "try" to pay attention by furrowing their brows, squinting, and straining their ears, and they can at least get a "B" for effort. We often continue to do this into adulthood, even though we know that this physical tension has nothing to do with being able to pay attention.

Starting a new habit often feels like effort, because we have to overcome years of bad habits. With our minds so full of past regrets, future worries, and current problems, it might seem a Herculean task to some people to keep their attention in the present moment.

Reality: Minds naturally wander. Many times, this is desirable, as this can lead to wonder and creativity. However, being more present in the moment can seem very difficult when our minds have been programmed to continuously look for what might go wrong, constantly ruminate about past mistakes, or to always be in a problem-solving mode.

The reality is that it takes a great deal more effort to struggle with our minds, emotions, and bodies than it does to notice the things as they are in the present. Mindfulness involves letting go of unnecessary effort (Kelly, 2019; Miller, 2014; Shapiro, Siegel, & Neff, 2018). When attempting to describe this in words, we create a paradox, because it can take an effort to let go of effort. Old habits can be deeply ingrained, and it can take effort to begin practicing a new way of being.

However, this effort does not have to feel like effort. Driving a car takes some effort, but tensely gripping the wheel adds unnecessary effort and actually interferes with your ability to drive efficiently. It takes focus to fly an airplane, but when I am taking off, pulling at my seat belt does not help to get the plane off the ground (Watts, 2004b).

Straining your muscles does not improve your ability to pay attention, because attention comes from brain processes, not muscular processes. If I ask you right now to take a "good hard look" at something, what do you experience? Most people will tense up their faces, eyes, brow, and bodies. Now, take a "soft look" at the same thing. Notice how "trying" to look at something does not help you see it any better.

"Trying" does not help to accomplish things and actually takes more effort than doing. Research has been done using scanners to compare the brain activity of those who practice mindfulness and those who do not when they are given difficult math problems. In the brains of those who practice mindfulness, there was activity only in the areas of the brain required to solve math problems. The brain scans of those who did not practice mindfulness were lit up like a Christmas tree—they were using too much unnecessary effort (Harrison, 2014).

Sometimes we think that to get better at something we have to put more and more effort into it, yet using less effort is often a key to mastery. An expert in any discipline is one who uses only the necessary amount of effort. In martial arts, beginners often tense up to force techniques to work. Yet, muscular strain impedes your ability to move freely, and it telegraphs what you are doing to your opponent. The expert martial artist moves like a ghost, impossible to feel, yet is as powerful as a hurricane.

Likewise, beginners often approach mindfulness practice as something that requires great effort, but they quickly discover that being present in the moment is the most natural thing in the world, and that the key is to let go of trying.

Of course, there is a big joke in all of this. People often say, "I need to try to be more in the moment," or "I've got to grab onto the present." The truth is, you can never get out of the present moment, whether you are trying or not trying. Whatever you do is happening right now. Even when you think about the past and the future, you are doing it now! The problem is that we too often confuse our thinking with what we are experiencing through our senses (Kabat-Zinn, 2005).

Summary: Many people think that learning mindfulness will take too much effort, but ruminating, worrying, and struggling with emotions all the time takes a great deal more effort. While creating a new habit can feel like it is taking effort, the fact is, you are already in the moment whether you notice it or not. The effort of trying creates unnecessary strain, because the truth is you cannot get out of the present moment.

Further Resources

Harrison, P. (2014). *The mindfulness movie* [DVD]. Where's My Mind? Media.

Kabat-Zinn, J. (2005). *Coming to our senses: Healing ourselves and the world through mindfulness.* Hachette UK.

Kelly, L. (2019). *The way of effortless mindfulness: A revolutionary guide for living an awakened life.* Sounds True.

Miller, L. D. (2014). *Effortless mindfulness: Genuine mental health through awakened presence.* Routledge.

Shapiro, S., Siegel, R., & Neff, K. D. (2018). Paradoxes of mindfulness. *Mindfulness, 9*(6), 1693–1701.

Watts, A. (2004b). *Out of your mind: Essential listening from the Alan Watts audio archives* [audio CD]. Boulder, CO: Sounds True.

Myth: Mindfulness can only be done sitting still. Some people believe that if you are not sitting still on the floor, you are not doing "real" mindfulness.

Basis in truth: People have engaged in contemplative practices for centuries sitting on the floor cross-legged. Often, this is preparation for longer absorption types of meditation, in which one shifts consciousness. When one's mind is one with the universe, the body needs to be in a stable position so that one can stay focused, and so that the body does not slump over.

Also, many ancient cultures did not use furniture like we have in modern times. It was simply normal to sit on the floor, and doing so did not require painful postures, because their bodies were used to it since birth.

Sitting still helps to reduce distractions, making it easier to practice paying attention when you begin to learn mindfulness. Many people have a habit of rushing around to accomplish things, programming their minds to be off in the future. Sitting still can be a helpful way to counter this compulsive tendency and to shift from a "doing mode" to a "being mode" (Teasdale, Williams, & Segal, 2014).

Reality: The debate on the importance of sitting mindfulness and meditation practice has gone on for centuries in some spiritual traditions, and arguments continue in modern times among mental health professionals and other researchers who study mindfulness. In the letters of Dahui Zonggao (Broughton & Watanabe, 2017), a 12th-century Zen teacher, he talks about sitting as a medicine provided in accordance with students' illnesses, and not as the goal. He warns students not to get stuck in "engirding-mind," not to get attached to their sitting, because the point of practice is to wake up to reality in the present moment.

There is a classic story of Zen master Mazu talking with a student who was sitting in meditation (Watts, 1957). When Mazu asked him why he was sitting in meditation, the student replied, "To become a Buddha." Mazu then picked up a tile and started polishing it. When the student asked him what he was doing, he said he was polishing it to make a mirror. "How can polishing a tile make a mirror?" asked the student. "How can sitting in meditation make a Buddha?" replied Mazu.

While sitting still has great value as a training device, it can sometimes become a fetish, something separate from daily life. It would be like insisting it was necessary to ride a bicycle with training wheels rather than take them off and ride freely. Buddhism speaks of the "four dignities" of humans: sitting, standing, walking, and lying down (Watts, 1957). One can be mindful in each of these postures.

Hence, formal mindfulness training programs, in both ancient and modern times, have incorporated mindful movement, such as walking and stretching, as well as instructions to be mindful during daily activities, like bathing, eating, and speaking with others (Boccio, 1993; Hanh & Anh-Huong, 2019; Kabat-Zinn, 2013).

Furthermore, there are certain individuals who have difficulty sitting still. People with anxiety, ADHD, Parkinson's disease, chronic pain, or a young child full of energy will not be interested in a program of sitting still. Such individuals might well benefit from beginning their mindfulness practices by paying attention during physical activities.

There was a time, before the proliferation of handheld electronic devices, when people would spend time just sitting on their porches. Most of us could probably benefit from more time sitting still. However, in modern society, we do not just sit around. We walk, drive, eat, have conversations, make love, and engage in countless other activities. Why would someone only want to pay attention when they are sitting still? All of our experiences can become richer if we bring more mindfulness into our moment-to-moment activities.

Summary: Sitting still can be a very useful mindfulness practice to help exercise one's capacity to pay attention and be present in the moment. However, the point is to take what one learns into more of the moments of everyday life. One can be mindful in any posture, and during any activity, even our seemingly humdrum, mundane daily chores. Life becomes much richer when we do so.

Further Resources

Boccio, F. J. (1993). *Mindfulness yoga: The awakened union of breath, body, and mind*. Simon and Schuster.

Broughton, J. L., & Watanabe, E. Y. (2017). *The letters of Chan Master Dahui Pujue*. Oxford University Press.

Hahn, T. N., & Anh-Huong, N. (2019). *Walking meditation: Easy steps to mindfulness*. Sounds True.

Kabat-Zinn, J. (2013). *Full catastrophe living: Using the wisdom of your body and mind to face stress, pain, and illness*, revised edition. Delta.

Teasdale, J., Williams, M., & Segal, Z. (2014). *The mindful way workbook: An 8-week program to free yourself from depression and emotional distress.* New York: Guilford Press.

Watts, A. (1957). *The way of Zen.* New York: Pantheon.

Myth: Mindfulness can only be done with eyes closed. Because mindfulness is often associated with other types of meditation, many people automatically think that one has to practice mindfulness with their eyes completely closed.

Basis in truth: In absorption-type meditations, in which one seeks to alter and broaden one's consciousness, the eyes are closed to reduce sensory input, because sensory stimulation tends to pull us into present moment reality. In visualization-type meditations, one closes one's eyes to facilitate the creation of a new reality through clearly picturing that desired reality in one's mind.

For many people, their attention easily wanders, and visual stimulation can trigger discursive thinking. When we see something, we can get caught up in all kinds of labels, thoughts, and memories about what we see. When first learning mindfulness, closing the eyes can be helpful to reduce distractions, especially when one begins to become more aware of internal experiences like bodily sensations, emotions, and thoughts.

Reality: While it can be helpful to practice with eyes closed in the beginning, a number of potential problems can arise if one rigidly believes the eyes must always be closed when practicing mindfulness.

For one, many people associate closing the eyes with going to sleep. Given that a majority of people in modern times are sleep deprived (American Psychological Association, 2014), this can be a major obstacle to being awake and present in the moment. If you do not get enough quality sleep, your body will grab some whenever it gets a chance. If you constantly rush around, your mind can be conditioned to immediately go to sleep when you close your eyes.

In addition, when the eyes are closed, many people have a tendency to create their own internal visualizations. We can inadvertently create artificial realties in our minds during mindfulness practice, rather than being present to the reality of our senses. Sensory input can only be experienced in the present moment.

Knowing that thoughts, labels, and memories come up automatically opens up an important lesson. Rather than shut our eyes and hope the thinking goes away, we can learn more about how our minds work. We can begin to tease apart the direct sensory stimulation from our thoughts about what we perceive. The word "sunset" does not do justice to the myriad of colors that one can see directly. It cannot be described adequately no matter how many words one uses, but it can be seen directly. We can use words out of convenience, but get less caught up in words, and we can learn not to mistake them for reality.

Perhaps most importantly, if you only practice with eyes closed, mindfulness begins to become dissociated from daily life. Once when I was teaching a workshop on mindfulness, someone told me that he can only practice mindfulness with his eyes closed. With a twinkle in my eye, I asked him, "How do you walk around without bumping into things? How do you drive a car? Are you mindless during those activities?" The whole point of practicing mindfulness is to bring more awareness into daily life, and most of us live our lives with eyes wide open.

One can practice mindfulness through all of the senses: the sense of touch through body sensations, taste through paying attention to eating, hearing through listening to environmental sounds, smell through noticing natural or incense scents, and seeing through looking around (Kabat-Zinn, 2005). Both traditional and modern mindfulness training programs often include a "mindfulness of seeing" exercise (Hahn, 2008; Kabat-Zinn, 2013; Teasdale, Williams, & Segal, 2014). Given that our analytical brains are automatically conditioned to connect thinking and memory to many artificial objects, it is often best to begin mindful seeing exercises using natural subjects, like trees, leaves, stones, or clouds. One can also practice mindful seeing through looking at or creating art, as in mindful doodling (Isis, 2016).

For people accustomed to only practicing with eyes closed, it can be a helpful transition to try practicing with the eyelids shaded, or partially closed, so that visual input is reduced but not eliminated.

Over time, the difference begins to blur between "practice" and daily life, and the brain is rewired to be more present whether eyes are open or closed (Kilpatrick, Suyenobu, Smith, Bueller, Goodman, et al, 2011; Sears, Bruns, Cotton, DelBello, Strawn, Kraemer, et al., 2021; Wong, Camfield, Woods, Sarris, & Pipingas, 2015).

Summary: Closing the eyes can be helpful when first learning mindfulness to reduce distractions. However, this can lead to sleepiness and mind wandering, so it can be helpful for beginners to experiment with keeping the eyes slightly open. Ultimately, the point of practice is to be more present in daily life with eyes wide open. Reality is what it is in this moment whether your eyes are open or closed, and clearly seeing will help you make wise choices and move toward what matters.

Further Resources

Hanh, T. N. (2008). *The miracle of mindfulness: The classic guide to meditation by the world's most revered master.* London: Rider.

Isis, P. (2016). *The mindful doodle book: Seventy-five creative exercises to help you live in the moment.* PESI Publishing and Media.

Kabat-Zinn, J. (2005). *Coming to our senses: Healing ourselves and the world through mindfulness.* Hachette UK.

Kilpatrick, L. A., Suyenobu, B. Y., Smith, S. R., Bueller, J. A., Goodman, T., Creswell, J. D., ... & Naliboff, B. D. (2011). Impact of mindfulness-based stress reduction training on intrinsic brain connectivity. *Neuroimage, 56*(1), 290–298.

Teasdale, J., Williams, M., & Segal, Z. (2014). *The mindful way workbook: An 8-week program to free yourself from depression and emotional distress.* New York: Guilford Press.

Wong, W. P., Camfield, D. A., Woods, W., Sarris, J., & Pipingas, A. (2015). Spectral power and functional connectivity changes during mindfulness meditation with eyes open: A magnetoencephalography (MEG) study in long-term meditators. *International Journal of Psychophysiology*, *98*(1), 95–111.

Myth: Mindfulness exercises have to be at least 45 minutes long.

Some people feel that mindfulness exercises have to be done for long periods of time, so they are just too busy to do them. Or, they might be afraid that even if they had the time to try them, opening up to all their thoughts and feelings for a long period of time would be overwhelming.

Basis in truth: One of the first structured mindfulness trainings to be scientifically studied was the eight-week MBSR program , which was first offered in the 1970s (Kabat-Zinn, 2013). In the program, Jon Kabat-Zinn gave each participant an audio cassette of mindfulness exercises to practice at home, many of which were 45 minutes long. These recordings are still available today (Kabat-Zinn, 2021). MBSR and similar programs have shown their effectiveness with a lot of research support over the years (de Vibe, Bjørndal, Fattah, Dyrdal, Halland, & Tanner-Smith, 2017; Querstret, Morison, Dickinson, Cropley, & John, 2020).

With physical exercise, it can be good to devote a specific amount of time to get into physical shape to overcome years of bad habits. Likewise, it can be good to devote a set length of time to practice mindfulness in order to develop new habits to overcome years of old, unhelpful habits of thinking and reacting.

Reality: There is debate as to how long a mindfulness exercise should be, and research results are mixed (Goldberg, Del Re, Hoyt, & Davis, 2014; Paulson, Huggins, & Gentile, 2019; Strohmaier, Jones, & Cane, 2021). While some studies show longer practice periods correlate with higher mindfulness ratings, other studies show the opposite.

It is difficult to argue with the wonderful research results of programs like MBSR. However, many individuals quit or are simply not interested in coming to a program that will require them to practice 45 minutes per day. For individuals with issues like high anxiety, or a history of trauma, the idea of opening up and becoming present to one's internal experiences for 45 minutes can sound terrifying. For this reason, many MBSR and other mindfulness programs offer differing lengths of mindfulness recordings for participants.

Jon Kabat-Zinn has recorded mindfulness exercises for the MBCT program that are 30 minutes long (Williams, Teasdale, Segal, & Kabat-Zinn, 2007). My own MBCT courses have only 15-minute exercises (psych-insights.com/mindfulness) and have been shown to produce effective results (Byerly-Lamm, 2017; Hente, Sears, Cotton, Pallerla, Siracusa, Spear Filigno, & Boat, 2020; Luberto, Wasson, Kraemer, Sears, Hueber, & Cotton, 2017; Sears, Tirch, & Denton, 2011).

Many studies have now confirmed that brief mindfulness exercises can be helpful, especially for beginners (Azam, Latman, & Katz, 2019; Basso, McHale, Ende, Oberlin, & Suzuki, 2019; Berghoff, Wheeless, Ritzert, Wooley, & Forsyth, 2017; Luberto & McLeish, 2018; Strohmaier, Jones, & Cane, 2021). In fact, an important component of the MBCT program is called the "three-minute breathing space" (Segal, Williams, & Teasdale, 2013; Williams, Teasdale, Segal, & Kabat-Zinn, 2007). When I teach the three-minute breathing space, people sometimes tell me they do not like it, because they need more time. With a teasing smile, I ask them, "So, you need more time to get into now?"

While longer mindfulness practices can be very helpful to develop attention and skill in working wisely with thoughts, feelings, and sensations, shorter exercises can be helpful to bridge formal practice with daily life. Even remembering to pause and take one mindful breath can be useful for breaking out of the habit of always living in our heads.

It appears that there is no one best length of practice time for everyone. What is best will likely be different from individual to individual. It also appears that practice quality may be more important than practice quantity (Goldberg, Del Re, Hoyt, & Davis, 2014).

Summary: Formal mindfulness exercises vary in how long they last, and it appears that there is no one best length of time that is optimal for all individuals. Ultimately, there is only this present moment, and you are already here, no matter how much "time" you take to try to get into it.

Further Resources

Basso, J. C., McHale, A., Ende, V., Oberlin, D. J., & Suzuki, W. A. (2019). Brief, daily meditation enhances attention, memory, mood, and emotional regulation in non-experienced meditators. *Behavioural Brain Research, 356,* 208–220.

Berghoff, C. R., Wheeless, L. E., Ritzert, T. R., Wooley, C. M., & Forsyth, J. P. (2017). Mindfulness meditation adherence in a college sample: comparison of a 10-min versus 20-min 2-week daily practice. *Mindfulness, 8*(6), 1513–1521.

Goldberg, S. B., Del Re, A. C., Hoyt, W. T., & Davis, J. M. (2014). The secret ingredient in mindfulness interventions? A case for practice quality over quantity. *Journal of Counseling Psychology, 61*(3), 491.

Kabat-Zinn (2021). *Guided mindfulness meditations: Series 1* [audio recording]. Mindfulnesscds.com.

Luberto, C. M., Wasson, R. S., Kraemer, K. M., Sears, R. W., Hueber, C., & Cotton, S. (2017). Feasibility, acceptability, and preliminary effectiveness of a 4-week Mindfulness-Based Cognitive Therapy protocol for hospital employees. *Mindfulness, 8*(6), 1522–1531. https://doi.org/10.1007/s12671 -017-0718-x

Sears, R., Tirch, D., & Denton, R. B. (2011). *Mindfulness in clinical practice* [with audio CD]. Sarasota, FL: Professional Resource Press.

Strohmaier, S., Jones, F. W., & Cane, J. E. (2021). Effects of length of mindfulness practice on mindfulness, depression, anxiety, and stress: A randomized controlled experiment. *Mindfulness, 12*(1), 198–214.

Williams, M., Teasdale, J. D., Segal, Z. V., & Kabat-Zinn, J. (2007). *The mindful way through depression: Freeing yourself from chronic unhappiness.* Guilford Press.

Myth: You must move slowly to be mindful. Some people think that in order to be mindful, they must move slowly, which does not seem practical in today's fast-paced world.

Basis in truth: Slowing things down is a wonderful way to practice mindfulness. Since we normally rush through the activities of daily life in an "automatic pilot mode," doing things slowly is a new experience that requires more attention, facilitating a shift from "doing mode" to "being mode" (Kabat-Zinn, 2013; Teasdale, Williams, & Segal, 2014).

When walking, people are usually rushing to get somewhere. If you slow down, walking becomes less automatic, and more attention is needed to maintain balance. You can begin to appreciate what a sophisticated activity walking really is. When you are no longer lost in your head, you can also remember that there is life, activity, and interesting things to see all around you while you are walking (Hahn & Anh-Huong, 2019; Kabat-Zinn, 2013).

When eating, people are often shoveling down their food in anticipation of the next bite. When you slow down your eating, it makes it easier to pay attention to all the subtleties of smell, taste, and texture in your food (Kristeller & Bowman, 2015).

You can turn almost any activity into a mindfulness practice by doing it at half speed. If you do anything at half speed, it becomes less automatic, and therefore easier to notice (Hayes, 2020b).

Reality: Mindfulness simply means paying attention, and one can pay attention no matter how fast one is moving (Kabat-Zinn, 2013; Sears, 2014). Slowing things down is a useful training exercise, and perhaps not a bad thing to do more often in life, but it is not required to pay attention and to be present in the moment.

You will drive more safely if you are mindful when driving a car, but you will not be safer driving only 10 miles per hour on the open highway. Even driving at full speed, you can practice paying attention to the road, the other drivers, and your surroundings.

I am quite mindful when I am flying an airplane, even though it is far more complicated than driving a car (operating in three dimensions rather than two). It is a wonderfully engaging activity, in which I can be fully present through all of my senses. Things can sometimes happen very quickly when flying, and if you have a habit of getting lost in ruminations or worries, you will be "behind the airplane." The avionics instruments and my sense experiences give me important information about how the aircraft is doing in the present. I can also balance lightly holding things in memory as well as planning and anticipating what is coming up next.

I have also learned a lot about mindfulness through martial arts training. It is very important to be present in the moment when someone is attacking you. Thinking about what you did wrong in the past or what you are going to do in the future will distract you from an effective response to what is unfolding in the moment. Unless you are practicing forms, as in tai chi, or rehearsing some new skills, it can be dangerous to purposely move slowly when you are being attacked. However, trying to move quickly can also get in the way. Efficiency and timing, fitting in with what the attacker is doing, is more important than speed. Learning to punch quickly actually required me to let go of unnecessary muscle tension.

When learning mindfulness, it can be helpful to start off moving slowly when doing an activity, then gradually increasing what you are doing to a normal speed. An interesting discovery one can make is that speed is relative. When one is fully present in the moment, things do not seem to fly by as quickly, because everything is happening now.

Summary: Performing activities slowly is a wonderful way to practice mindfulness, because it is a simple way to break up automatic habits. However, since mindfulness is simply paying attention in the moment, one can be mindful when doing any activity at any speed.

Further Resources

Hahn, T. N., & Anh-Huong, N. (2019). *Walking meditation: Easy steps to mindfulness*. Sounds True.

Hayes, S. C. (2020). *ACT immersion: An introduction to ACT as a process-based therapy* [Online Video Course]. https://act.courses/signup/

Kabat-Zinn, J. (2013). *Full catastrophe living: Using the wisdom of your body and mind to face stress, pain, and illness*, revised edition. Delta.

Kristeller, J., & Bowman, A. (2015). *The joy of half a cookie: Using mindfulness to lose weight and end the struggle with food*. New York: Perigee.

Sears, R. (2014). *Mindfulness: Living through challenges and enriching your life in this moment.* London, UK: Wiley-Blackwell.

Teasdale, J., Williams, M., & Segal, Z. (2014). *The mindful way workbook: An 8-week program to free yourself from depression and emotional distress.* New York: Guilford Press.

5 Myths about the Magical and Mystical Effects of Mindfulness Practice

The popularity of movies about superheroes suggests a desire for many to have (or at least experience vicariously) superhuman powers. Because it is unlikely that a person will be bitten by a radioactive spider or will receive an invitation to a wizarding school, some people want to practice mindfulness in the hopes that it might give them special powers.

Very often these desires are present in order to escape unpleasant feelings, distressing thoughts, or difficult life circumstances. However, after practicing mindfulness, one comes to understand that, in a sense, being fully present in this moment is the most special power one could ever develop.

In this chapter, we will explore myths about mindfulness and extrasensory perception, magic, mystically becoming one with the universe, discovering the meaning of life, and about secret, advanced forms of mindfulness.

Myth: Mindfulness gives you ESP or magical powers. Some people are motivated to practice mindfulness because they believe it will give them extrasensory perception or other magic powers.

Basis in truth: If you are present in the moment, you will be more fully aware of sense impressions. The senses can only be experienced in the present moment—everything else is thinking, imagination, or memory. To people who are always lost in worries and ruminations, those who are able to pay close attention to the senses may seem to have extrasensory perception.

If you spend most of your time inside your mind, when you encounter people who are fully present in their senses, they may seem magical. For example, expert musicians are not lost in thinking, they are present in their senses, allowing their fingers to move almost magically to produce beautiful music. Analytical thinking can get in the way of the free flow of playing.

Reality: Those who practice mindfulness do not necessarily have ESP or magical powers. However, it can appear so to those who are dominated by verbal thinking. The human brain can do far more than think in words. When you get out of your own way, you can tap into those other brain perceptions and functions (Siegel, 2007).

My fifth-degree ninja black belt test in To-Shin Do was all about getting out of my own way and trusting myself (Hayes, 2013; Sears, 2014). I had to stand with my back to my teacher, Stephen K. Hayes, who was standing behind me with an upraised practice sword. The sword does not cause permanent damage, but it can sure sting if it hits. When performing this test, the teacher can strike you almost immediately or might just stand there for several minutes before striking. If you get hit, you fail. If you move before the teacher swings, you also fail.

How do you pass a test in which your back is to a sword that can drop on your head at any moment? The last thing you want to do is get caught up in your thinking. If you are carried away with worries about how much it might hurt, or what other people will think if you fail, you will not be present. Even if you are thinking about trying to pick up on hearing the sword moving you will fail, because by the time you think you hear it, it is too late to move. Your thinking mind is at least 500 milliseconds behind reality. In other words, when you consciously think something, the reality and initial brain activity is at least half a second before that (Libet, Gleason, Wright, & Pearl, 1983). An interesting fact to think about.

If you are an athlete, you know that you cannot pause to consciously think about what to do if, for example, a tennis ball is flying straight at you. When you first learn tennis, you of course slowly practice the nuances of how to swing a racket, which your brain processes in the premotor cortex. Through lots of practice and overrepetition, the motor sequences become encoded in deeper structures within the brain known collectively as the basal ganglia (Carlson & Birkett, 2021).

Of course, all my intellectual knowledge of how the brain works was of little use as I was standing there waiting for a sword to slam down on my head. I was simply able to temporarily allow my thinking to settle, resting in the moment without really caring whether or not I would be hit, and it felt like my body got pulled to the side as the sword came down.

I do not necessarily think that I have any kind of ESP or magical powers. Perhaps my brain picked up on some cues of which I was not consciously aware, processing and analyzing them in the background. Maybe my brain sensed a shift in air pressure as my teacher moved. Perhaps I actually did hear movement, but I did not stop to think about it and trusted my brain to move me. I could swear that a few times when practicing for this test, I could smell underarm deodorant as the teacher raised his arms. I would not overly rely on such a skill (so please do not try to hit me in the back of the head if you see me), but it is quite an interesting experience to practice getting out of my own way. The test represents a significant shift in ninja training from reliance on verbal thinking to one of being more open to a much wider range of subtleties.

An expert in any discipline is one who has learned to pay attention to sense cues in the moment by letting go of preconceived notions and who allows the mind to function more fully.

Summary: In comparison to someone who is often caught up in mental representations, those who practice mindfulness can appear to sense things that others do not sense and to be able to do things that seem magical. In reality, such individuals are more tuned into their senses in the present moment, and they know that their minds and bodies are truly magical if they do not interfere with their natural functioning.

Further Resources

Hayes, S. K. (2013). *The complete ninja collection.* Black Belt Communications.

Libet, B., Gleason, C. A., Wright, Jr, E. W., & Pearl, D. K. (1983). Time of conscious intention to act in relation to onset of cerebral activity (readiness-potential). *Brain, 106,* 623–642.

Sears, R. (2014). *Mindfulness: Living through challenges and enriching your life in this moment.* London, UK: Wiley-Blackwell.

Siegel, D. J. (2007). *The mindful brain: Reflection and attunement in the cultivation of well-being (Norton series on interpersonal neurobiology).* WW Norton & Company.

Myth: Mindfulness is a mystical practice that makes you one with the universe. Some people practice mindfulness because they are unhappy with their daily lives and want to pursue a mystical state. At the opposite extreme, some people choose not to learn about mindfulness because they are not interested in mystical states.

Basis in truth: There are definitely moments in mindfulness practice when one feels connected to everything in the universe. It is a profound realization that language itself creates distinctions that do not exist in the real world. If you are asked to point to the difference between my fingers, rather than to describe any differences in words, you will realize that "difference" itself is an idea and has no concrete existence in the world of the senses (Watts, 1957). When words and thoughts fall away, this reality can be experienced directly. My Zen teacher's teacher was fond of saying, "When you are not thinking, there is no difference between you and me" (Seung Sahn, 1997).

From a certain perspective, boundaries do not separate us, they join us (Watts, 1965). My skin does not separate me from the atmosphere, it connects me to it. Even at a purely scientific level, we are interconnected with the entire universe, in both major and subtle ways (Sears,

2017a). We share air, water, and even atoms with other living beings through respiration and consumption in order to survive. We need heat and light from the sun, air from the trees and diatoms, and iron in our blood from exploding stars in order to exist at all. In a sense, we are the entire universe experiencing itself at the point we call "I."

There are certain types of practices known as absorption meditations designed to purposefully bring about this sense of oneness with the universe. This state of consciousness can be produced through a series of graduated concentrative exercises or through repetitious activities such as chanting, as in Transcendental Meditation (Yogi, 1963). Mindfulness is often a foundational or preparatory practice for absorption meditations, as they require a strong attentional capacity.

Brain scan research has even discovered specific neurological activity correlated with the feeling of oneness with the universe that comes about when practicing absorption meditation (D'Aquili & Newberg, 1999; Newberg, d'Aquili, & Rause, 2008). A region in the parietal lobe of the brain that has been dubbed the orientation association area (OAA) is associated with spatial perception. In one brain hemisphere, the OAA region gives us the feeling of what is us, generally at the boundary of the skin. The other hemisphere tells us what is not us or what is outside us. The fact that our brains make these distinctions has survival value. It is useful for navigation, so that we do not bump into things, and helps us tell the difference between what is our hand and what is food.

However, when one is in the state of absorption meditation, the brain activity levels in both OAA regions diminish greatly, and they stop communicating with each other. Imagine what that would feel like—to no longer be able to distinguish what is "me" from what is "outside me." This is why people report feeling "one with the universe." It is a literal description of their subjective experience.

Of course, one cannot remain rapt in absorption indefinitely. Eventually, one must rise out of that meditative state and interact with others, eat food, and earn a living. All those activities require attention in the present moment.

Reality: Mindfulness is often confused with absorption-type meditations, but they have different purposes. Mindfulness is simply paying attention in the present moment and is not necessarily about shifting to a mystical state of consciousness.

Mindfulness practice fosters present moment awareness. Interestingly, the late Alan Watts (2010) called mysticism "ecological awareness," referring to an ability to directly perceive all of our interconnections and interdependence with our environment. After all, we cannot exist separate from the universe in which we come to exist and from which we are nourished. When you pay attention, you simply become more aware of this.

Unfortunately, there are some people who seek to become one with the universe to escape from dealing with their daily lives. If done in this spirit, the attempt to escape can become a pattern of compulsive avoidance of reality, which can lead to endless cycles of struggle.

Likewise, if you want to become one with the universe to feel better about yourself, you may eventually realize you are really just doing so to aggrandize your ego. As Alan Watts (2011) observed, the biggest ego trip going is the game to get rid of your ego. If you realize that you are truly one with the universe, you see that there is no one with whom to compete. The ego is just an idea, a useful fiction, since there is no you that can exist independently of everything else.

It may seem obvious, but where else could you be but here and now? Where else can you possibly go? You may have an idea about where you want to go in the future, but you can only take each step in the present moment. As the title of one of Jon Kabat-Zinn's (2009) books says, wherever you go, there you are.

After seeing the wonder of all of our interconnections, how amazing it is that you have come to be in this moment, reading these words that I am sharing with you.

Summary: Mindfulness is about paying attention. There are times when one recognizes and feels a connection with one's environment and all other living beings, but the main purpose is to be present in this moment, the only place one can ever be.

Further Resources

Kabat-Zinn, J. (2009). *Wherever you go, there you are: Mindfulness meditation in everyday life*. Hachette Books.

Newberg, A., d'Aquili, E. G., & Rause, V. (2008). *Why God won't go away: Brain science and the biology of belief*. Ballantine Books.

Sears, R. (2017). *The sense of self: Perspectives from science and Zen Buddhism*. New York: Springer Nature.

Seung Sahn (1997). *The compass of Zen*. Shambhala Publications.

Watts, A. (2011). *Eastern wisdom, modern life: Collected talks: 1960–1969*. New World Library.

Watts, A. (1957). *The way of Zen*. New York: Pantheon.

<u>Myth: Mindfulness gives you the meaning of life.</u> Many people feel they are stuck in a boring, mundane existence and long for something beyond daily life. Some hope that mindfulness can give their lives meaning.

Basis in truth: If you pay close attention, you will come to experience that this moment is all that exists. When you experience reality empirically, that is, through your senses, you can begin to realize that the past and future are only ideas. While they can be useful ideas, they have no concrete physical reality. You cannot perceive the past or the future through your senses—you cannot hear the future, and you cannot touch the past. To the senses, only the present moment exists (Kabat-Zinn, 2005).

Through mindfulness practice, people often come to recognize that they have spent almost their entire lives living in their heads, ruminating about the past or worrying about the future. When you let go of mentally created ghosts and come fully into this present moment, it can feel like you have finally found meaning.

Reality: Mindfulness is just the process of paying attention. It does not tell you what matters or what to do. It cannot "give" meaning.

The problem of finding meaning turns out to actually be a problem of semantics. Words have meaning—they point to something beyond themselves (Watts, 1957). They are symbols or sounds that represent something else. The word "water" represents a certain liquid reality. The word is very useful if I am thirsty, and I ask someone for a bottle of water. But I cannot drink the word "water." The word itself is only a sound or a set of letters on a page that represents something else. However, if I am touching that liquid reality, and I ask what it means, I am confusing the water with words.

When you look at a sunset, what does it mean? It is a beautiful phenomenon that we experience directly with our senses. It does not mean anything, because it does not represent something other than itself.

If we ask, "What is the meaning of life?," we are confusing a word with our lived experiences. Asking what "life" means is a meaningless question.

Of course, it is only human to desire to have purpose, to have things to look forward to in life. Some people wander through life hoping that purpose and meaning will fall from the sky and drop onto their heads. However, since meaning does not exist outside of one's own thinking, many would argue that one creates one's own meaning (Frankl, 1985; Hayes, Strosahl, & Wilson, 2012; Yalom, 1980).

Mindfulness can be a useful tool in this endeavor by helping us tease apart what is truly fulfilling for us from what is unquestioned conditioning or old habit. By paying attention, we can consciously choose what is important, and then engage in behaviors in the present moment that move us toward those chosen values. For example, if family is meaningful and fulfilling to me, I can choose small actions each day to nurture my connection to family, rather than only thinking about family in an abstract or symbolic way.

Summary: The attempt to "find" meaning in life is a confusion of words with reality. However, with mindfulness practice, one can more clearly decide what one wishes to do in the moments that constitute one's life, and therefore can have a life that is more fulfilling and meaningful.

Further Resources

Frankl, V. E. (1985). *Man's search for meaning*. Simon and Schuster.

Hayes, S. C., Strosahl, K., & Wilson, K. G. (2012). *Acceptance and commitment therapy: The process and practice of mindful change*, 2nd edition. New York: Guilford Press.

Kabat-Zinn, J. (2005). *Coming to our senses: Healing ourselves and the world through mindfulness*. Hachette UK.

Watts, A. (1957). *The way of Zen*. New York: Pantheon.

Yalom, I. D. (1980). *Existential psychotherapy*. Basic Books.

Myth: There are secret, advanced forms of mindfulness. Mindfulness just sounds too simple to some people. They think they must be missing something. They believe that there might be something secret, something being held back. They think there must be something more advanced, more profound, for which mindfulness training is preparing them.

Basis in truth: In the mainstream media, mindfulness is often portrayed in an overly simplistic way, such as breathing to feel calmer. Actual mindfulness practice, and especially how it can be applied to issues arising in daily life, is much more sophisticated. In that sense, how to apply it to complicated problems, like anxiety and grief, may seem secret or advanced.

In formal mindfulness training programs, such as MBSR (Kabat-Zinn, 2013) and MBCT (Segal, Williams, & Teasdale, 2013), students begin with very simple mindfulness exercises, such as paying attention to the breath or scanning one's body to notice physical sensations. Practicing these simple techniques helps to build attentional capacity. Later exercises become more subtle, such as listening to sounds, noticing thoughts, and even purposefully bringing attention to difficult experiences, memories, and physical pain. These exercises might be considered more advanced, because if you have trouble paying attention to your own breath, it is likely to be very difficult to pay attention to challenging experiences without spiraling off into old, unhelpful habits of ruminating, worrying, or distracting.

One could perhaps say that in the sense that they are not as publicly available, some mindfulness practices are secret but accessible. For example, there is a practice known as "choiceless awareness" (Kabat-Zinn, 2013; Krishnamurti, 2000; Milton, 2011). This practice is not often taught to beginners by most mindfulness teachers, because it does not make logical sense to someone without experience in mindfulness practice. It involves being present and aware without focusing on any particular sense impression. In a similar sense, even though books on quantum physics are publicly available, they are very difficult to understand without extensive training and guidance from physics professors.

Thirty years ago, I was initiated into the Japanese Vajrayana Buddhist tradition known as *mikkyo*, which literally means "secret teachings" (Hayes, 2019). This tradition gave certain teachings only to initiates because of their potential to be misunderstood. The students were assessed to ascertain if they were ready and mature enough to know certain things about human nature. Knowledge can be both powerfully used as well as misused. Information about sex, for example, can lead to wonderful, blissful intimacy with another human being, but such knowledge can be useless or even harmful to children before they are old enough and ready for such an experience.

Likewise, mental health professionals agree to follow legal and ethical guidelines in the application of psychological interventions, including mindfulness-based treatments. In fact, using mindfulness with certain mental health disorders can create more problems if not done competently. A protocol manual for how to use mindfulness in the treatment of PTSD is publicly available (Sears & Chard, 2016), but there are "secrets" in how to apply it in the sense that it can be very helpful to have training and guidance from someone who has experience working with trauma. Individuals with PTSD often develop the habit of avoiding or suppressing their unpleasant memories, thoughts, and emotions. Asking them to learn to relate to these experiences with kindness and compassion can be challenging if not done carefully. If done incorrectly, mindfulness can even make some clients worse.

Reality: People often feel there is something missing. That if only they had it, then everything would be okay. It could be money, relationships, the right teacher, books, or any number of things. I once collected books as if just owning them meant I would be smarter and suffer less.

My Zen teacher Wonji entitled one of his books, "You think it is a secret, but it never has been one" (Wonji Dharma, 2011). It turns out the real secret is that everything is clearly in front of you if you pay attention.

Mindfulness is very simple. Just pay attention in this moment. It is our thinking which makes things complex. Can you explain in words how to open and close your hand? And yet it is so simple to do.

Of course, simple and easy are not always the same thing. Martial arts is simple. I can summarize 40 years of training in how not to be hurt by an attacker in one sentence: Do not occupy the same space at the same time as the attacker's weapons. Obviously not an easy thing to do consistently.

In fact, I have learned more about mindfulness from martial arts than from any other training method. The more advanced I got, the more aware I became of my thoughts, feelings, and body sensations from moment to moment, as well as those of the attacker. What to do with that awareness is where all the training and experience comes in.

Playing guitar is another example of something being very simple but not necessarily easy. It is just plucking strings in sequence while moving your fingers along the frets. However, with such simple movements can come marvelously sophisticated and beautiful music, as long as one is willing to do the hard work of practice.

Likewise, mindfulness, or paying attention in the present moment, is very simple. There is no hidden secret. Yet, how it is applied in one's daily life, or to mental health challenges, can seem quite advanced. What you choose to do with this simple present moment can be marvelously complex and fascinatingly beautiful.

I have been asked on a number of occasions to teach an "advanced mindfulness" course. It is very interesting to explore what people mean by this. How can there be an "advanced" way to be present in this moment, the only time and place you can ever be? Yet, there are certainly subtle aspects that are often missed by people with a superficial understanding of mindfulness practice.

Unfortunately, this seeking for "advanced" or "secret" teachings can cause you to constantly look for something which has always been right in front of your face. Zen teachers have frequently emphasized the importance of having a "don't know mind" (Seung Sahn, 1999) or a "beginner's mind" (Suzuki, 2020). The mind of a beginner is always wide open to possibilities, but experts often have a tendency to only notice a narrow range of what is possible.

Incidentally, after being guided for years in the *mikkyo* secret teachings through all manner of complex and sophisticated practices, do you know what the biggest "secret" was? Just to be present in the moment. Below is a loose translation from a secret commentary for a complicated ritual I was given:

> *Although these categories are created to explain things, ultimately, all individual categories are false. The six great elements, the four mandalas, the three secrets, and so forth, do not really exist. Those categories are aids. They are devices used for the sake of practice. In the secret teachings, the practice itself is the end. This is the same idea as in mindfulness practice. Therefore, the accomplished practitioner is able to discard these categories and the devices they contain, and simply be awake in each moment.*

Summary: There are a number of mindfulness practices that are not as well known publicly, so one could consider them secret in that sense. Some practices are a bit more challenging than others, and so may be considered more advanced. However, mindfulness is in fact very simple—consciously noticing one's experiences in the present moment. Our thinking is what tends to obscure reality and to make things more complicated than they are.

Further Resources

Hayes, S. K. (2019). *Action meditation: The Japanese diamond and lotus tradition*. Nine Gates Press.

Kabat-Zinn, J. (2013). *Full catastrophe living: Using the wisdom of your body and mind to face stress, pain, and illness*, revised edition. Delta.

Sears, R., & Chard, K. (2016). *Mindfulness-based cognitive therapy for PTSD*. London, UK: Wiley-Blackwell.

Segal, Z., Williams, M., & Teasdale, J. (2013). *Mindfulness-based cognitive therapy for depression*, 2nd edition. New York: Guilford Press.

Seung Sahn (1999). *Only don't know: Selected teaching letters of Zen Master Seung Sahn*. Shambhala Publications.

Suzuki, S. (2020). *Zen mind, beginner's mind*. Shambhala Publications.

Wonji Dharma. (2011). *Wu Shan Lu five mountain record*. Buddha Dharma University Press.

6   Myths about Mindfulness and Mental and Physical Health

Despite all the technological advances of humankind and of the medical professions, people continue to suffer from a variety of mental and physical health issues. To some, mindfulness offers hope for dealing with these issues, and many studies are showing promising results. Those who are desperate for health, or who feel like their lives are flying by, are attracted to myths about seemingly miraculous cures and even to the possibility of extending the human lifespan.

In this chapter, we will explore myths about mindfulness and the brain, mental health, chronic pain, medical conditions, and longevity.

Myth: Mindfulness completely rewires the brain. Some people are unhappy with how their brains are operating and hope to quickly rewire the entire brain with a little mindfulness.

Basis in truth: Numerous studies of those who practice mindfulness are now showing that there are detectable changes in the structure and functioning of the brain (Hanson & Mendius, 2009; Hölzel, Lazar, Gard, Schuman-Olivier, Vago, & Ott, 2011; Siegel, 2007; Tang, Hölzel, & Posner, 2015). One of the most interesting findings is that the mPFC gets thicker after an eight-week MBSR course (Lazar, Kerr, Wasserman, Gray, Greve, Treadway, et al., 2005). The nine functions of this area of the brain are discussed below.

Nine Functions of the mPFC: In his book *The Mindful Brain*, Daniel Siegel (2007) talks about the nine functions of the mPFC. While the frontal lobes as a whole are associated with general executive functions like planning, decision-making, and impulse control, the mPFC in particular plays a role in some very important functions.

Body Regulation

Even though the brain stem is largely responsible for general life support and body regulation, the mPFC sends nerve fibers down to that area to modulate some of these functions. Even vagal tone, which was once thought to be set at birth, appears to improve with meditative practices such as loving-kindness (Kok, Coffey, Cohn, Catalino, Vacharkulksemsuk, et al., 2013; Vestergaard-Poulsen, van Beek, Skewes, Bjarkam, Stubberup, et al., 2009).

Attuned Communication

In our modern age filled with technological distractions, many people display a "lights are on but nobody's home" appearance. Individuals who practice mindfulness develop the ability to be completely present and tuned into the person with whom they are talking. During my time as a bodyguard for the Dalai Lama, I experienced his ability to make you feel like you were the only person in the world in the moment when he caught your gaze, even when surrounded by a crowd of thousands. My challenge was to subtly break this connection with members of the crowds so we could move him to the next venue.

Emotional Balance

While the limbic system is primarily responsible for emotions, the mPFC sends nerve fibers down to modulate the feelings that arise. While you still feel the full range of emotions, training in mindfulness helps to tone down the intensity of emotional signals so they are less overwhelming and more appropriate to the situation.

Response Flexibility

When we are overwhelmed by our emotions, we tend to become less flexible. We retreat into old patterns of thinking, emotional reactions, and behavioral habits. Becoming more flexible means that we are better able to notice how things are and make conscious responses to situations rather than automatic reactions. Instead of letting our feelings alone drive our choices, we make conscious decisions about what we want to do in difficult situations.

Empathy

Empathy is the capacity to relate to what other people are feeling. We know that certain individuals, like those with antisocial personality disorder, have a diminished capacity for empathy, which is why they are more easily able to harm others emotionally and even physically. In fact, such individuals have been found to have 11% less gray matter in the prefrontal cortex (Raine, Meloy, Bihrle, Stoddard, et al., 1998; Raine, Lencz, Bihrle, LaCasse, et al., 2000). While this can be an advantage in dangerous careers like military combatant or police officer, we know that having empathy enriches our relationships.

Insight or Self-Knowing Awareness

It can be challenging for many of us to recognize our own thoughts, behaviors, and emotional states. We can act and react so automatically that we do not realize the impact we have on others. When we practice mindfulness, we increase our capacity to notice our internal states and develop the ability to more consistently "step back" and see the big picture of how our actions and words affect the people and the environment around us.

Fear Modulation

The amygdala, which is part of the limbic system, plays a major role in generating the fear response. However, the mPFC basically sends fibers down to modulate feelings of fear. In people who practice mindfulness, the fear response tends to be less overwhelming and tends to pass more quickly (Strawn, Cotton, Luberto, Patino, Stahl, et al., 2016).

Intuition

One might not expect to see a word like intuition on a scientific list about the brain. In this context, intuition does not necessarily imply ESP or something mystical, but gets at the fact that the human brain is capable of doing much more than our consciousness knows. We tend to identify the sense of self with our verbal thinking (Sears, 2017a), which processes information in a serial, linear fashion. However, the brain uses parallel processing, continuously taking in information, doing background analyses, and synthesizing data all throughout the day and night. When your conscious thoughts begin to settle down, you can become more open and trusting of your own brain. While that does not necessarily mean you should make major life decisions based solely on hunch, you do tend to become open to a deeper sense of knowing.

When we are not off thinking compulsively in our heads, there are times when we are fully present with another human being, and we pick up on things that we would ordinarily miss. We might do or say something that is right on target, perhaps even surprising ourselves and the other person that we could possibly have known or said such a thing. Perhaps your olfactory centers picked up on something subtle, like the smell of sweat from their nervousness, so you had a sense that the person was stressed. Perhaps your emotional centers picked up on how the person was really feeling despite the words they were using and their best attempts to hide their emotions from you (and maybe even from themselves). When your mind is less dominated by compulsive thinking, it is easier to get out of your own way.

Morality

Morality is also an unusual word to see on a scientific list. Morality here does not necessarily mean an externally imposed code of behavior. Looking over the list above, when individuals are more attuned in their communications with others, less overwhelmed by their emotions and fears, more flexible in their behavior, more empathic with others, and more insightful about themselves, they are probably more likely to be considerate of others in their daily lives.

Brain Studies in Children: Brain studies of children and mindfulness have been much less common, but my colleagues and I have made some pioneering steps (Cotton, Luberto, Sears, Strawn, Wasson, & DelBello, 2015; Strawn, Cotton, Luberto, Patino, Stahl, et al., 2016). Our initial study performed fMRI scans of 10 children with anxiety disorders, who also had at least one parent with bipolar disorder, before and after the 12-week Mindfulness-Based Cognitive Therapy for Children protocol (MBCT-C: Semple & Lee, 2011). After the mindfulness training, the children had increased activation in the bilateral insula, lentiform nucleus, thalamus, and left anterior cingulate while viewing emotional stimuli, structures that subserve interoception and the processing of internal stimuli. Also, increased scores on a measure of mindfulness were correlated with decreased amygdala activity during fear processing. In other words, practicing mindfulness allowed these youths to become more aware of body sensations, yet they were less affected when they were shown fearful images.

We also performed fMRI scans on kids with mood dysregulation after completing MBCT-C (Sears, Bruns, Cotton, DelBello, Strawn, et al., 2021). Even when people are "doing nothing," the brain still fires in certain patterns known as "resting state networks" (Smith, Fox, Miller, Glahn, Fox, et al., 2009). Fascinatingly, even when these children were "doing nothing," their brains were firing more actively in areas related to interoception. In other words, the scans suggest that even when they are not actively practicing mindfulness, they are more in their bodies and less caught up in worry and rumination in their daily lives.

Reality: While these and many other brain studies show truly remarking findings, the actual changes are quite small. In fact, they are practically undetectable in any individual human being. The changes are currently only found by applying computerized statistical analysis using composite data collected from multiple subjects.

All of the qualities of the mPFC described above are on a continuum. Through mindfulness practice, one may become a little more empathic, but one does not necessarily go from coldhearted to saintly after an eight-week program. The results seen also require regular daily practice, not just a few minutes a day.

To say that mindfulness completely rewires the brain is an exaggeration. At the opposite end of the continuum, every thought, sense impression, and experience you have creates small changes in the brain. One of the benefits of these research studies is to show that mindfulness practice really does have a concrete, tangible effect on specific brain areas.

Summary: There is much truth in this myth, but as with many other myths, there is much exaggeration to say that the brain is completely rewired. The brain changes created by mindfulness practice are indeed measurable, but compared to the entire brain, are small and subtle. Of course, to any given individual, those small changes can make a big difference in their daily lives.

Further Resources

Hanson, R., & Mendius, R. (2009). *Buddha's brain: The practical neuroscience of happiness, love & wisdom*. Oakland, CA: New Harbinger Publications.

Hölzel, B., Lazar, S., Gard, T., Schuman-Olivier, Z., Vago, D., & Ott, U. (2011). How does mindfulness meditation work? Proposing mechanisms of action from a conceptual and neural perspective. *Perspectives on Psychological Science, 6*(6) 537–559. DOI: 10.1177/1745691611419671

Lazar, S. W., Kerr, C. E., Wasserman, R. H., Gray, J. R., Greve, D. N., Treadway, M. T., . . . Fischl, B. (2005). Meditation experience is associated with increased cortical thickness. *Neuroreport, 16*(17), 1893–1897.

Siegel, D. J. (2007). *The mindful brain: Reflection and attunement in the cultivation of well-being (Norton series on interpersonal neurobiology)*. WW Norton & Company.

Strawn, J., Cotton, S., Luberto, C., Patino, L., Stahl, L., Weber, W., Eliassen, J., Sears, R., & DelBello, M. (2016). Neurofunctional changes associated with mindfulness-based cognitive therapy in anxious youth at risk for developing bipolar disorder. *Journal of Child & Adolescent Psychopharmacology, 26*(4), 372–379. DOI: 10.1089/cap.2015.0054

Myth: Mindfulness cures mental disorders. Because mindfulness is such a common part of modern psychotherapy interventions, some people hope that just by practicing mindfulness all their mental health issues will disappear.

Basis in truth: Mindfulness is now a common intervention in clinical practice (Baer, 2015; Sears, Tirch, & Denton, 2011), and mindfulness and acceptance-based therapies are considered the "third wave" of CBT (Sears, 2017b).

There are a growing number of structured, well-researched eight-week psychological interventions using mindfulness. The first to be developed, in the 1970s by Jon Kabat-Zinn (2013) and colleagues, is MBSR. It was primarily designed to help with stress and chronic pain but has been applied to a wide variety of mental health issues. Segal, Williams, & Teasdale (2013) adapted the MBSR program into MBCT, which was originally designed to prevent relapse of depression, though it now has also been applied to a wide variety of issues. Other eight-week programs are customized for specific populations, like MBCT-C (Semple & Lee, 2011), Mindfulness-Based Cognitive Therapy for Posttraumatic Stress Disorder (Sears & Chard, 2016), Mindfulness-Based Relapse Prevention for Addictive Behaviors (Bowen, Chawla, Grow, & Marlatt, 2021), Mindfulness-Based Eating Awareness Training (Kristeller & Bowman, 2015; Kristeller & Wolever, 2011), Mindfulness-Based Relationship Enhancement (Carson, Carson, Gil, & Baucom, 2004), Mindfulness-Based Childbirth and Parenting (Duncan & Bardacke, 2010), and Mindfulness-Based Elder Care (McBee, 2008). A longer-term program that incorporates a significant mindfulness component is Dialectical Behavior Therapy (Linehan, 2015a, b, 2020), originally designed to be used for Borderline Personality Disorder. A full-service psychotherapy intervention with decades of research support that incorporates mindfulness is ACT (Hayes, 2005; Hayes, Strosahl, & Wilson, 2012).

These and other mindfulness-based approaches have been shown to be helpful for a wide variety of mental health issues, including addiction (Bowen, Chawla, Grow, & Marlatt, 2021; Luberto & McLeish, 2018; Paulson, Huggins, & Gentile, 2019), anxiety (Blanck, Perleth, Heidenreich, Kröger, Ditzen, et al., 2018; Sears, 2021), bipolar disorder (Cotton, Kraemer, Sears, Strawn, Wasson, et al., 2019; Lovas & Schuman-Olivier, 2018), depression (Luberto, White, Sears, & Cotton, 2013; Williams, Teasdale, Segal, & Kabat-Zinn, 2007), personality disorders (Sng & Janca, 2016), posttraumatic stress disorder (O'Bryan, Kraemer, Luberto, & Sears, 2019; Sears & Chard, 2016), and thought disorders (Khoury, Lecomte, Gaudiano, & Paquin, 2013).

Not surprisingly, research shows that mindfulness is helpful for clinicians' own stress and mental health (Davis & Hayes, 2011; Fulton, 2005; Hente, Sears, Cotton, Pallerla, Siracusa, Spear Filigno, & Boat, 2020; Irving, Dobkin, & Park, 2009; Kraemer, Wasson, Lyle, Wu, Sears, et al., 2015; Luberto, Wasson, Kraemer, Sears, Hueber, & Cotton, 2017; Shapiro, Astin, Bishop, & Cordova, 2005; Shapiro, Brown, & Biegel, 2007). Also, when clinicians practice mindfulness, their patients tend to have better outcomes (Grepmair, Mietterlehner, Loew, Bachler, Rother, & Nickel, 2007). In addition, because mindfulness appears to enhance empathy and strengthen the therapeutic relationship (Hick & Bien, 2008; Wexler & Ott, 2006), the likelihood of being sued for malpractice may decrease (Beckman, Markakis, Suchman, & Frankel, 1994; Huntington & Kuhn, 2003). While citing these studies can help convince administrators to give their clinicians mindfulness training, it should be a no-brainer that when clinicians pay attention, their patients tend to do better, and they are less likely to be unhappy with their providers.

Reality: As with the previous myth about brain research, there is a lot of truth in this myth, but its claims are exaggerated. The amount of research showing how helpful mindfulness can be is truly stunning, but just doing mindfulness alone does not "cure" a person of all mental disorders.

Many factors contribute to mental health, including genetics, epigenetics, nutrition, physical exercise, environmental stressors, social support, and self-care. Since mindfulness is just paying attention, it can be a very useful tool to maintain mental health.

Mindfulness is just one component of effective mindfulness-based psychological treatments. Psychologists and other mental health professionals receive years of supervised training to competently treat mental health disorders. There are wonderful mindfulness teachers who have had no training in working with clinical disorders and very competent clinicians who have only dabbled in mindfulness practice. While each may be competent in doing what they are good at doing, problems arise when someone tries to combine mindfulness and psychotherapy without sufficient training. For example, people with posttraumatic stress disorder often work hard to suppress their strong memories and emotions, so opening up to those experiences must be done in a careful, conscious way. If mindfulness is used to help the individual "feel better" in the short run, it could inadvertently reinforce avoidance, making the condition worse in the long run (Sears & Chard, 2016).

Summary: Thousands of research studies have shown that psychological interventions utilizing mindfulness are very effective at treating a wide variety of mental health disorders. However, mindfulness is only one component of even mindfulness-based interventions. Paying attention alone does not create mental health, though it can be a very useful tool for helping to maintain a variety of factors that contribute to mental well-being.

Further Resources

Baer, R. A. (Ed.). (2015). *Mindfulness-based treatment approaches: Clinician's guide to evidence base and applications.* Elsevier.

Bowen, S., Chawla, N., Grow, J., & Marlatt, G. A. (2021). *Mindfulness-based relapse prevention for addictive behaviors: A clinician's guide*, 2nd edition. New York: Guilford Publications.

Cotton, C., Kraemer, K. M., Sears, R. W., Strawn, J. R., Wasson, R. S., Welge, J., Blom, T. J., Durling, M. & DelBello, M. P. (2019). Mindfulness-based cognitive therapy for children and adolescents with anxiety disorders at-risk for bipolar disorder: A psychoeducation waitlist controlled pilot trial. *Early Intervention in Psychiatry; 1–9.* Doi: https://doi.org/10.1111/eip.12848

Hayes, S. C. (2005). *Get out of your mind and into your life: The new acceptance and commitment therapy.* New Harbinger Publications.

Kristeller, J., & Bowman, A. (2015). *The joy of half a cookie: Using mindfulness to lose weight and end the struggle with food.* New York: Perigee.

Sears, R. (2017). *The cognitive-behavioral therapy and mindfulness toolbox.* Eau Claire, WI: PESI Publishing & Media, Inc.

Sears, R., & Chard, K. (2016). *Mindfulness-based cognitive therapy for PTSD.* London, UK: Wiley-Blackwell.

Sears, R. (2021). *ACT with anxiety: An acceptance and commitment therapy workbook to get you unstuck from anxiety and enrich your life.* Eau Claire, WI: PESI Publishing & Media, Inc.

Sears, R., Tirch, D., & Denton, R. B. (2011). *Mindfulness in clinical practice.* Sarasota, FL: Professional Resource Press.

Williams, M., Teasdale, J. D., Segal, Z. V., & Kabat-Zinn, J. (2007). *The mindful way through depression: Freeing yourself from chronic unhappiness.* Guilford Press.

<u>Myth: Mindfulness always eliminates chronic pain.</u> Chronic pain is a serious, debilitating problem for millions of people around the world. When traditional medicine fails, frustrated individuals turn to alternative interventions like mindfulness, hoping it will get rid of all their pain.

Basis in truth: When Jon Kabat-Zinn (2013) first designed MBSR back in the 1970s, he was creating a program to help a broad variety of individuals with daily life stress. As the program went on, Dr. Kabat-Zinn found himself working more and more with individuals suffering from chronic pain. Over the decades, he and other researchers have fine-tuned mindfulness techniques and principles to help individuals with pain issues. Dr. Kabat-Zinn (2010) has even created mindfulness recordings specifically for those suffering from chronic pain.

Though the results of individual studies may vary, meta-analyses of mindfulness-based interventions do indeed show some benefits to those with chronic pain (Bawa, Mercer, Atherton, Clague, Keen, et al., 2015; Hilton, Hempel, Ewing, Apaydin, Xenakis, et al., 2017; Veehof, Trompetter, Bohlmeijer, & Schreurs, 2016).

Reality: Pain is a complicated phenomenon. It has both physical and psychological components, which interact with and affect each other. When operating properly, the pain system is supposed to acclimate to a steady stimulus, readjusting itself to a new normal (Carlson & Birkett, 2021). Unfortunately, a number of things can interfere with this readjustment, including one's own stress response to the pain, which can create internal struggles with thoughts, emotions, and muscular tension.

Mindfulness definitely does not always eliminate chronic pain. While the meta-analyses of mindfulness-based interventions for pain do show some benefits, the improvements are not much different from other treatments for chronic pain.

When pain is constant and intense, we can forget that we actually need pain. In an extremely rare genetic condition known as congenital insensitivity to pain, or congenital analgesia, a person is born without the ability to feel pain (Drissi, Woods, & Woods, 2020; Schon, Parker, & Woods, 2020). Unfortunately, these individuals tend to have a short lifespan, because they do not notice when their bodies are damaged or ill, and therefore do not take action to get help.

Because pain is by definition unpleasant, people tend to make it an enemy. They forget that pain is simply a messenger, giving us information. Through mindfulness practice, we can become more compassionate with ourselves. After all, pain is due to issues within our own bodies, and cursing, getting angry at, and tensing up against our own bodies only increases suffering.

As Kabat-Zinn and others emphasize, the goal is not to completely get rid of pain but to create a life worth living, even if there is pain within your life (Dahl & Lundgren, 2006; Kabat-Zinn, 2013; Linehan, 2020).

Summary: Meta-analyses of mindfulness-based intervention for chronic pain can be helpful for many individuals, but mindfulness does not always eliminate chronic pain. Chronic pain can have a wide variety of causal and maintaining factors. Mindfulness can be useful to help one change one's relationship to pain, so that one can create a life worth living even with chronic pain.

Further Resources

Dahl, J., & Lundgren, T. (2006). *Living beyond your pain: Using acceptance & commitment therapy to ease chronic pain*. New Harbinger.

Kabat-Zinn, J. (2010). *Mindfulness meditation for pain relief: Guided practices for reclaiming your body and your life* [audio CD]. Boulder, CO: Sounds True.

Kabat-Zinn, J. (2013). *Full catastrophe living: Using the wisdom of your body and mind to face stress, pain, and illness*, revised edition. Delta.

Linehan, M. M. (2020). *Dialectical behavior therapy in clinical practice*. Guilford Publications.

Veehof, M. M., Trompetter, H. R., Bohlmeijer, E. T., & Schreurs, K. M. G. (2016). Acceptance-and mindfulness-based interventions for the treatment of chronic pain: A meta-analytic review. *Cognitive Behaviour Therapy, 45*(1), 5–31.

Myth: Mindfulness cures medical diseases and makes you live a much longer lifespan. Many people are motivated to practice

mindfulness in the hopes that it will cure an illness or that it will help them live much longer.

Basis in truth: Many studies have been conducted on the usefulness of mindfulness with medical diseases such as high blood pressure, autoimmune diseases, and cancer. Meta-analyses have shown that mindfulness can be helpful for clients with these and other medical conditions (Bohlmeijer, Prenger, Taal, & Cuijpers, 2010; Gotink, Chu, Busschbach, Benson, Fricchione, & Hunink, 2015; Grossman, Niemann, Schmidt, & Walach, 2004; Ledesma & Kumano, 2009). Meta-analyses of studies done with patients with hypertension have even shown measurable drops in blood pressure after mindfulness training (Intarakamhang, Macaskill, & Prasittichok, 2020; Scott-Sheldon, Gathright, Donahue, Balletto, Feulner, et al, 2020).

Fascinatingly, studies have also shown that mindfulness increases telomerase activity, an enzyme which repairs telomeres, a genetic marker related to healthy aging and longevity (Epel, Daubenmier, Moskowitz, Folkman, & Blackburn, 2009; Schutte & Malouff, 2014).

Reality: The benefits of mindfulness for patients with medical issues are indeed very promising, but it is not a miracle cure. The research actually seems to suggest that mindfulness practice is useful for coping with and managing the psychological effects of medical issues, not necessarily for eliminating them, and the meta-analyses show great diversity in how helpful mindfulness practice is to any given individual with medical conditions (Black & Slavich, 2016).

More detailed research is needed to tease apart all the factors at play for each medical problem, because there are many factors that contribute to physical health and longevity, such as genetics, epigenetics, environment, physical exercise, and stress (Clark, 1998). Medical issues can be very stressful, and stress affects the immune system. Stress can increase the functioning of the immune system too much, as in autoimmune disorders, or stress can overwhelm the immune system, reducing its functioning. Hence, stress can make one more vulnerable to disease or can interfere with the body's natural ability to heal (Sapolsky, 2004). It may well be that its stress-reducing effect is one of the reasons mindfulness is helpful for medical issues (Black & Slavich, 2016). Stress also affects telomere length, so the effects of mindfulness on longevity may also be due to its potential to reduce stress reactions (Etzel & Shalev, 2021; Von Zglinicki, 2002).

While more research is necessary on the direct effects of mindfulness on medical issues, it is obvious that it can be beneficial to pay attention when one has a medical condition that requires proactive decision-making and care strategies. If one lives consciously in the moment, letting go of stressful struggles with one's own thoughts, feelings, and body sensations, one will have more quality moments in life regardless of the quantity of time one has.

Summary: While mindfulness is not a miracle cure, and more research is necessary on the direct physiological effects, individuals with a variety of medical conditions can indeed benefit from mindfulness practice. As an adjunct treatment, mindfulness shows great promise for reducing stress and developing the ability to make conscious care decisions. Whether or not it appreciably extends lifespan, mindfulness can definitely help to improve one's quality of life by helping one to live more fully in each moment.

Further Resources

Bohlmeijer, E., Prenger, R., Taal, E., & Cuijpers, P. (2010). The effects of mindfulness-based stress reduction therapy on mental health of adults with a chronic medical disease: A meta-analysis. *Journal of Psychosomatic Research, 68*(6), 539–544.

Epel, E., Daubenmier, J., Moskowitz, J. T., Folkman, S., & Blackburn, E. (2009). Can meditation slow rate of cellular aging? Cognitive stress, mindfulness, and telomeres. *Annals of the New York Academy of Sciences, 1172*, 34.

Gotink, R. A., Chu, P., Busschbach, J. J., Benson, H., Fricchione, G. L., & Hunink, M. M. (2015). Standardised mindfulness-based interventions in healthcare: An overview of systematic reviews and meta-analyses of RCTs. *PloS One, 10*(4), e0124344.

Grossman, P., Niemann, L., Schmidt, S., & Walach, H. (2004). Mindfulness-based stress reduction and health benefits: A meta-analysis. *Journal of Psychosomatic Research, 57*(1), 35–43.

Intarakamhang, U., Macaskill, A., & Prasittichok, P. (2020). Mindfulness interventions reduce blood pressure in patients with non-communicable diseases: a systematic review and meta-analysis. *Heliyon, 6*(4), e03834.

Ledesma, D., & Kumano, H. (2009). Mindfulness-based stress reduction and cancer: a meta-analysis. *Psycho-Oncology: Journal of the Psychological, Social and Behavioral Dimensions of Cancer, 18*(6), 571–579.

Schutte, N. S., & Malouff, J. M. (2014). A meta-analytic review of the effects of mindfulness meditation on telomerase activity. *Psychoneuroendocrinology, 42*, 45–48.

7 Myths about Mindfulness in Daily Life and Work

There are many myths surrounding if or how mindfulness might be applied in one's daily life and work. Some individuals believe that mindfulness is only a lofty spiritual practice, an escape from the chores of daily life, and therefore should not be sullied by being applied to mundane day-to-day tasks. Others may hope that mindfulness will magically make them happy in all of their daily routines. Even corporations have been promoting mindfulness among employees, with both hopes and fears about its effects on efficiency and productivity.

In this chapter, we will explore several myths about mindfulness in work settings and daily life: that it can only be done in peaceful settings, that one must be mindful at all times, that one will become unfeeling and lose compassion, that one will forget appointments and responsibilities, that it takes years to be mindful, that mindfulness interferes with work, and that it is hard to find time to be mindful.

Myth: You can only be mindful in a peaceful setting. Some people feel that mindfulness can only be done on a mountaintop or in a temple, and therefore is not applicable to their busy lives, their work environment, or to things like raising children.

Basis in truth: For thousands of years, certain individuals have chosen to go off into secluded places in nature to engage in contemplative practices. They voluntarily forego relationships and financial worries to follow spiritual pursuits. Mindfulness is a common practice on the spiritual path (Gunaratana, 1996; Sears, 2014).

On a much smaller scale, those who begin learning mindfulness are often advised to find a peaceful setting in which to practice. Since a big part of mindfulness is learning to hone one's attentional capacity, it can be helpful in the beginning to reduce distractions by finding a quiet, undisturbed space in one's home. Natural settings are also helpful, because trees and clouds do not usually pull for automatic ruminations, worries, and problem solving (Lymeus, Lundgren, & Hartig, 2017; Nisbet, Zelenski, & Grandpierre, 2019). Since Earth and sky do not require intellectual analysis, it becomes easier to be present to the beauty of a sunset, the smell of the air, and the feeling of the breeze on one's face.

Reality: It is easy to be peaceful on a mountaintop, but for many of us, we enjoy the challenge of living a full life with all the richness and messiness that come with engaging in a productive work life and in having relationships with other human beings and animals (Kabat-Zinn, 2013).

Mindfulness is simply about being more present in our moments. Whether sitting, standing, walking, or lying down, we can develop the habit of actually being in our lives, rather than compulsively living in our heads. We can choose more often to notice our present experiences rather than being lost in a past that cannot change or a future that exists only in thought. For many people, when they are at work, they are thinking about being at home with family, and when they are at home with family, they are thinking about doing something fun, and when they are doing something fun, they are thinking about work.

While of course we would all prefer to live in a beautiful natural setting, you can be present in any moment. When in the mountains, enjoy the cool air and the wind whispering through the beautiful trees. When in a traffic jam in the city, enjoy the lights and the cacophony of voices and car horns.

You can be fully present even in the midst of a terrible crisis. If you were rushed into an emergency room, and blood was spurting from your body, you would not want the ER attending physician to shout,

"Oh no, I'm feeling upset; excuse me while I go to a peaceful place and calm down!" You would want the physician to be fully present in the moment while they were taking care of you, even if they were having anxious feelings or thoughts about being sued for malpractice.

Ultimately, even "distractions" are events happening in the present moment. What are you seeing, hearing, feeling, smelling, and tasting right now? Just this.

Summary: Practicing mindfulness in a peaceful setting is ideal for developing skills in mindfulness, and being in nature can be inspiring and rejuvenating. However, since mindfulness is simply paying attention, we can bring that awareness into all of our moments, so that we can be more present when we drive a car, spend time with our families, or deal with crises at work.

Further Resources

Gunaratana, B. H. (1996). *Mindfulness in plain English, revised and expanded edition*. Wisdom Publications.

Kabat-Zinn, J. (2013). *Full catastrophe living: Using the wisdom of your body and mind to face stress, pain, and illness*, revised edition. Delta.

Lymeus, F., Lundgren, T., & Hartig, T. (2017). Attentional effort of beginning mindfulness training is offset with practice directed toward images of natural scenery. *Environment and Behavior, 49*(5), 536–559.

Nisbet, E. K., Zelenski, J. M., & Grandpierre, Z. (2019). Mindfulness in nature enhances connectedness and mood. *Ecopsychology, 11*(2), 81–91.

Sears, R. (2014). *Mindfulness: Living through challenges and enriching your life in this moment*. London, UK: Wiley-Blackwell.

Myth: It is important to be mindful at all times. Some people believe that the goal of mindfulness practice is to be always completely aware of everything. They try very hard to keep their attention in the present moment.

Basis in truth: Since so many of us in modern society are raised to focus on the future, it can be a wonderful feeling of relief to allow ourselves to be fully present in this moment. Life becomes so much richer, and even dealing with crises becomes simpler when we are present to things as they are actually happening from moment to moment.

In the beginning, it can take effort to get into the present, because our minds are so conditioned to be ruminating about the past and worrying about the future. However, when you stop trying to get into the moment, you realize that you have always been in the moment. Where else you could you be? Even when you are thinking about the past and the future, you are doing it now. You are in the moment at all times.

Reality: You are in the moment at all times, but you may not be aware of all of your sense impressions in the moment at all times. I'm a Zen master, and I have known many Zen masters, and we are not always mindful.

It is impossible for human beings to always be completely aware. In any given moment, there are countless things of which one could be aware. As I am writing this, I hear the fan on my laptop softly humming, digging sounds from a construction crew outside, cars passing by, birds chirping, my daughter talking, and a soft ringing sound in my ears. It would take the rest of this book to even begin to describe all the feelings throughout my body and all the sights within my field of view. While I can be fully present to all this just as it is, there is no need to force myself to try to consciously hold all these things in awareness.

It is important to note that there is an arousal component to attention (Hölzel, Lazar, Gard, Schuman-Olivier, Vago, & Ott, 2011; Jha, Krompinger, & Baime, 2007; Kinomura, Larsson, Gulyas, & Roland, 1996; Posner & Rafal, 1986; Sears, Tirch, & Denton, 2011). While attention does not require muscle tension, it does take a little bit of brain energy to focus, which is why stimulants like caffeine improve attention, and why sedatives and alcohol decrease attention. Therefore, you would not want to try to pay attention all the time. It is perfectly fine to zone out and take vacations sometimes, as long as it is done purposefully in the right situation.

My Zen teacher Wonji Dharma told me a story about his teacher (who was also the teacher of Jon Kabat-Zinn, [2005]), Zen Master Seung Sahn, that illustrates this point. When Seung Sahn first came to the United States from Korea, he did not speak the language, so he would teach in broken English, saying things like, "When eating, just eat. When walking, just walk." In fact, long before Nike adopted the slogan, he would say, "Just do it!" (Seung Sahn, 1997). In other words, be present in what you are doing, instead of always lost in your head as so many of us tend to be. One day, the Zen master was sitting in the Zen Center, eating his breakfast while reading the newspaper. A student walked in and said, "Great Teacher! You have always told us, 'When eating, just eat,' yet here you are, eating and reading the newspaper!" Without skipping a beat, Seung Sahn looked up and said, "Oh! When eating and reading the newspaper, just eat and read the newspaper!"

Sometimes making mindfulness a special "thing" undermines the whole point of it. I remember once sharing a retreat space with another group of Zen students who were trying hard to notice every bite of food in the lunchroom. They scowled at my friends and me when one of us made a joke and we laughed out loud. It is wonderful to be present, but there is no need to force it and use it as a weapon of superiority.

I often tell my overachieving students not to go overboard with this paying attention stuff. After all, if you are present in about 5% of your life right now, wouldn't it be great to be present about 10% of the time? You could double your life experiences!

Summary: Although one is always in the present moment, there are far more sensory impressions happening than anyone can be consciously aware of at any given time. The effort to try to constantly be aware actually gets in the way of being in touch with this present moment, the only place one can ever really be.

Further Resources

Hölzel, B., Lazar, S., Gard, T., Schuman-Olivier, Z., Vago, D., & Ott, U. (2011). How does mindfulness meditation work? Proposing mechanisms of action from a conceptual and neural perspective. *Perspectives on Psychological Science, 6*(6) 537–559. DOI: 10.1177/1745691611419671

Jha, A. P., Krompinger, J., & Baime, M. J. (2007). Mindfulness training modifies subsystems of attention. *Cognitive, Affective, & Behavioral Neuroscience, 7*(2), 109–119.

Kabat-Zinn, J. (2005). *Coming to our senses: Healing ourselves and the world through mindfulness*. Hachette UK.

Sears, R., Tirch, D., & Denton, R. B. (2011). *Mindfulness in clinical practice*. Sarasota, FL: Professional Resource Press.

Seung Sahn (1997). *The compass of Zen*. Shambhala Publications.

Myth: If you become too mindful, you will become unfeeling and lose compassion for others. This myth is the opposite of the one above, believing that bad things will happen if you become too mindful. Since some people think mindfulness is being blissed out, they fear that it might make them stop caring about other people.

Basis in truth: As discussed in Chapter 2, there are certain types of meditations in which an individual comes to feel a oneness with the universe. Traditional meditative traditions talk about the two perspectives of "absolute" reality and "relative" reality (Hayes, 2019). From the relative perspective, we see things from the inside out. We look around at our environment and notice how all these seemingly disparate things and beings interact with and affect each other. We root for ourselves and have to battle against what might harm us.

From an absolute perspective, we see things from the outside in. We can see the big picture workings of the universe. From an astronomical perspective, we can see that billions of galaxies, each containing billions of stars and planets, are wonderfully harmonious, and the daily struggles of individual human beings are quite miniscule and insignificant in this context.

Likewise, if you look closely at the workings of your own internal bodily systems, there are tremendous battles going on continuously between microorganisms. Yet if you were to kill all the microorganisms in your body, you would die. From a bigger perspective, these battles are part of being a healthy human being. In this sense, what is seen as conflict from a relative point of view can be seen as harmony from an absolute point of view (Watts, 2005).

Alan Watts (2021) talks about some of the traps which can befall someone who stumbles across different states of consciousness without knowing how to interpret them. One is called the "plastic doll," in which everyone around you seems to be made of plastic, mere automatons with no life inside. On the other hand, you can also see everything, even inanimate objects, as full of life and energy, and as manifestations of processes that are connected to the entire universe.

Reality: There are times when mindfulness practice leads to a sense of connection with all things and allows glimpses of the absolute perspective. However, the primary purpose is to pay attention, which can only happen in the present moment through embodiment in the relative world.

It can be useful to explore what people mean by being "too mindful." If by that expression someone means they are putting forth a lot of effort all the time, then it will indeed create problems, as discussed in the previous myth. However, some people may fear being "too mindful" because it can sometimes seem easier to remain in old habits of blissful ignorance. Becoming more mindful actually involves opening up the senses as well as the heart. Paying attention allows us to see how interconnected we are with the world around us and all the beings with whom we share it.

In fact, people who practice mindfulness actually have increased compassion (Germer, 2009; McKay & Walker, 2021; Neff & Germer, 2018; Salzberg, 2002, 2011; Tirch, Schoendorff, & Silberstein, 2014). A number of studies have shown that mindfulness and self-compassion are highly correlated (Birnie, Speca, & Carlson, 2010; Hollis-Walker & Colosimo, 2011; Kuyken, Watkins, Holden, White, Taylor, et al., 2010; Neff, 2003). After all, the more you notice your own thoughts, feelings, and sensations without battling with them, the kinder you become with yourself. By paying attention and recognizing that all human beings share similar struggles, you develop more compassion for others as well.

Ultimately, you can come to realize that there is no real distinction between absolute and relative reality. Each individual being is the entire universe manifesting itself in a particular time and place. You therefore come to feel compassion for all individual beings while also knowing we are all connected as a whole.

Summary: There are certain types of meditations in which one can glimpse a kind of higher order of harmony in the universe, and from this perspective, individual lives can seem insignificant. However, mindfulness is about paying attention in the moment. Through awareness of habitual ways that we tend to struggle with our own thoughts and feelings, we can let go of those struggles and be more compassionate with ourselves. Through recognition of our connections and shared struggles with others, we are more likely to develop compassion for all beings.

Further Resources

Germer, C. (2009). *The mindful path to self-compassion: Freeing yourself from destructive thoughts and emotions.* Guilford Press.

Hayes, S. K. (2019). *Action meditation: The Japanese diamond and lotus tradition.* Nine Gates Press.

McKay, T., & Walker, B. R. (2021). Mindfulness, self-compassion and wellbeing. *Personality and Individual Differences, 168,* 110412.

Neff, K., & Germer, C. (2018). *The mindful self-compassion workbook: A proven way to accept yourself, build inner strength, and thrive.* Guilford Publications.

Salzberg, S. (2002). *Lovingkindness: The revolutionary art of happiness.* Shambhala Publications.

Tirch, D., Schoendorff, B., & Silberstein, L. R. (2014). *The ACT practitioner's guide to the science of compassion: Tools for fostering psychological flexibility.* New Harbinger Publications.

Watts, A. (2005). *Do you do it, or does it do you?.* Sounds True.

Myth: If someone is mindful, they will forget appointments and responsibilities. Some people believe that if you become "too" present in the moment, you will forget to pay your bills and will not be able to function in society.

Basis in truth: Most of us are conditioned to think that all the good things in life are coming in the future. We go to school for many years, then try to advance in the workplace, then live for retirement. There are certain individuals who have become disillusioned by the idea that everything will be better in the future, and end up going to the other extreme, deciding not to make a lot of plans.

Similarly, from a young age, we are told we must be responsible, and some people rebel against this when they get older. There are some meditators who enjoy getting lost in meditative states, because it is much more pleasant than the responsibilities of daily life. There are some who want to get lost in what they are doing now in order to avoid dealing with reality.

Reality: In my workshops, I am commonly asked, "What about people who are *too* in the moment? What about keeping up with life responsibilities?" In my experience, such people are not really fully in the moment. They are usually avoiding dealing with difficult things in their lives and use "being in the moment" as an excuse. They may seem to be naturally present, but they are actually avoiding responsibility. For example, an individual may feel anxiety about getting a job, so tries to get lost "in the moment" playing video games.

I have never met someone who is "*too* in the moment." I spent a little time with the Dalai Lama and with about a dozen Zen masters, and they can be present in the moment but still attend to their responsibilities. If the moment requires you to go to an appointment or to take care of something, you just go to take care of things in that moment.

One of the aims of mindfulness practice is actually to take greater responsibility for one's life choices (Alkoby, Pliskin, Halperin, & Levit-Binnun, 2019; Ludwig & Kabat-Zinn, 2008; Small & Lew, 2019). Awareness of how things are, and of your own thoughts and feelings, helps you to make a clear, conscious choice rather than an automatic reaction.

Once you are aware, an important question becomes, what do you want to be responsible for? What matters do you? What is really important? (Hayes, 2005). Mindfulness can help you clarify what your values really are. You can then choose to make plans to do what matters.

The reality is I can make plans for the future in this moment. However, compulsively ruminating about the future only increases anxiety and does not accomplish anything in the present moment. There is no end to future possibilities one can worry about. Sadly, if your present moments are always full of future worries, you will miss all your present moments and your life will fly by (Kabat-Zinn, 2009). Since the future is only an idea (you cannot see it, feel it, touch it, smell it, or taste it), you are always in the present moment. Even when you are thinking about the future, you are doing it now.

The difference between getting lost in or making use of the concept of the future lies in consciously choosing to make or not make plans. I can regularly check my planner and make notes about appointments and what is most important to do, but I do not have to make plans all day long at the expense of not experiencing my life as it is unfolding.

Summary: There are some who claim to be fully in the moment, but who do so to avoid taking responsibility or dealing with unpleasant realities. When you are mindful, you pay attention to what matters, and therefore become more response-able, or responsible. Your ability to make plans and keep appointments can actually enrich your present moments.

Further Resources

Alkoby, A., Pliskin, R., Halperin, E., & Levit-Binnun, N. (2019). An eight-week mindfulness-based stress reduction (MBSR) workshop increases regulatory choice flexibility. *Emotion*, *19*(4), 593.

Hayes, S. C. (2005). *Get out of your mind and into your life: The new acceptance and commitment therapy*. New Harbinger Publications.

Kabat-Zinn, J. (2009). *Wherever you go, there you are: Mindfulness meditation in everyday life*. Hachette Books.

Ludwig, D. S., & Kabat-Zinn, J. (2008). Mindfulness in medicine. *JAMA*, *300*(11), 1350–1352.

Small, C., & Lew, C. (2019). Mindfulness, moral reasoning and responsibility: Towards virtue in ethical decision-making. *Journal of Business Ethics*, 1–15.

Myth: It takes years to become mindful. Many of us have been so programmed to live in our heads, constantly worrying about the future or ruminating about the past, that becoming capable of fully living in the present seems a monumental task. Many people even keep running logs of how many hours they practice.

Basis in truth: Evolutionary processes have favored those who can learn from the past and plan for the future, so our brains have a natural tendency to do so (Hayes, 2020a; Hayes, Strosahl, & Wilson, 2012). We also spend years going through educational systems that teach us to learn from history and work hard for the future (Watts, 1958). It can take years to shift those brain circuits.

Some people measure their success in mindfulness by counting the number of hours they have sat in meditation, which a friend of mine irreverently refers to as the "ass-ometer." Certain teacher groups even ask for this number to be admitted into their clubs. This is understandable, as it can be hard to find objective measures to know about an individual's skill in mindfulness.

Reality: What color are these words that you are reading right now? What sounds do you hear around you? What do you feel in your body?

You were just mindful. Mindfulness is simply paying attention in the present. You are already here in this moment, so it does not have to take years to be able to notice that. Where else could you be but here and now?

In a few minutes, your brain may revert to deeply ingrained, automatic habits of getting lost in old thought patterns. However, each time you bring your attention back to this moment, you are reinforcing new brain pathways (Lazar, Kerr, Wasserman, Gray, Greve, Treadway, et al, 2005; Siegel, 2007).

The Korean Zen teacher Chinul talked about "sudden awakening, gradual cultivation" (Buswell, 1991). Whether or not we formally practice mindfulness, we have all had experiences of "waking up," or feeling fully present and content in the moment. However, since most of us have been programmed to live primarily in our heads, we have old habits and conditioning that pull us back into compulsive thoughts about the future and the past. It does take time and conscious intention to gradually cultivate changes in the brain to return to our natural, innate ability to be more fully present more consistently.

While experience can be very important, unfortunately, number of hours does not always equate with expertise. As an example, for airplane pilots, initial experience is important to develop skill, but beyond 1,000 hours of flight time, more experienced pilots do not necessarily have fewer accidents (Ison, 2005; O'Hare, Chalmers, & Scuffham, 2006).

In the realm of psychotherapy, I have known therapists who are fantastically great at what they do right after they get licensed, likely due to a combination of great training and high intrinsic ability. However, I have also met therapists who have been practicing longer than I have been alive but who are able to do very little for their clients.

Practice does not make perfect, perfect practice makes perfect (Hayes, 2013). What you practice is what you become. When someone sits down and sets a timer, how are they spending that time? In fact, research suggests that quality of mindfulness practice is more important than quantity (Goldberg, Del Re, Hoyt, & Davis, 2014).

Remember that you become what you expose your mind to. If you are frequently exposed to others who are constantly rushing around in their minds, you are more likely to do so as well. You are in this moment now. And if you consciously make time to practice mindfulness, it becomes easier and more natural.

Summary: Number of hours spent sitting does not necessarily equal ability to be present. Anyone can be mindful in this very moment. However, practice can help to solidify and strengthen that ability. Quality of practice appears to be more important than quantity.

Further Resources

Buswell Jr, R. E. (1991). *Tracing back the radiance: Chinul's Korean way of Zen.* University of Hawaii Press.

Goldberg, S. B., Del Re, A. C., Hoyt, W. T., & Davis, J. M. (2014). The secret ingredient in mindfulness interventions? A case for practice quality over quantity. *Journal of Counseling Psychology, 61*(3), 491.

Hayes, S. C. (2020a). *A liberated mind: How to pivot toward what matters.* Avery.

Hayes, S. C., Strosahl, K., & Wilson, K. G. (2012). *Acceptance and commitment therapy: The process and practice of mindful change*, 2nd edition. New York: Guilford Press.

Hayes, S. K. (2013). *The complete ninja collection.* Black Belt Communications.

Siegel, D. J. (2007). *The mindful brain: Reflection and attunement in the cultivation of well-being (Norton series on interpersonal neurobiology).* WW Norton & Company.

Watts, A. (1958). *Nature, man and woman.* Pantheon Books.

<u>Myth: Mindfulness interferes with your ability to work.</u> Despite the fact that mindfulness trainings are becoming increasingly common in corporate and workplace settings (Badham & King, 2019), some believe that such training is a waste of time at best and may even interfere with one's ability to be a productive manager or employee.

Basis in truth: Our stress can motivate us to be productive, so that we can get our work done and not be fired. When we pause and check in, we might realize that our work often does not really call for the life and death struggle that the stress system is designed to deal with. We may even question if the work we are doing is really worthwhile in an existential sense, and so we may feel less motivation to complete that work (Hafenbrack & Vohs, 2018).

Studies have also shown that if your job requires you to fake your emotions, like salespeople, servers, or customer service representatives, being more aware of your emotions on the job can create distress (Lyddy, Good, Bolino, Thompson, & Stephens, 2021).

Reality: Though studies of mindfulness in the workplace have sometimes had mixed results, the majority of research studies support that mindfulness improves employee well-being and mental health, reduces stress, increases job satisfaction, reduces burnout, improves work performance, and improves attention and task focus (Johnson, Park, & Chaudhuri, 2020; Vonderlin, Biermann, Bohus, & Lyssenko, 2020; Walsh & Arnold, 2020).

One of the keys to understanding how mindfulness can be helpful at work is to understand how important attention is. As we know from neuropsychology research, there are different types of attention, and each one uses varying brain pathways (Sohlberg & Mateer, 1989). Interestingly, all of these types of attention are exercised in mindfulness practices.

Focused attention is the ability to place your attention where you want it. This can be narrow, as when looking very carefully at one of the letters on this page, or broad, as when you are driving a car and need to focus on your surroundings. Sustained attention is the ability to keep your attention where you want it. Selective attention involves choosing what to attend to and what to ignore in the presence of competing stimuli. Alternating attention involves shifting one's attention between a variety of stimuli. All of these types of attention are useful and important in the workplace.

Mindfulness practices also exercise our capacity for divided attention, though most of us already do it too much, in ways that are not helpful. In general, multitasking tends to increase the time it takes to complete a task, because the brain has to keep shifting sets when it jumps to different tasks, increasing processing time (Adler & Benbunan-Fich, 2012; Otto, Wahl, Lefort, & Frei, 2012). I once taught in a graduate business program, and one of my students told me that one of his other professors helped him experience the drawbacks of multitasking directly. The class was divided into two groups. The professor gave each group five different kinds of tasks to do. The students on one side of the room were told to try to do all of the tasks at the same time as fast as they could. The students on the other side were asked to do each task one at a time as fast as they could. The individuals who did the tasks one at a time got them done in half the amount of time as the individuals who tried to do them at the same time.

It strikes me as quite amusing how often you see "must be good at multitasking" in job advertisements. It is basically saying, "You must be good at doing things that are stressful and inefficient in order to fit into our organizational culture."

Of course, there are times when divided attention is a very important skill, as when driving a car or flying an airplane. If you get overly focused on just one thing when you are operating a vehicle, you are likely to crash. Each workplace can experiment with how and when to apply each type of attention.

It is common in busy workplaces for employees to have high levels of distress about carrying too many tasks in their minds. A psychologist who was employed in a busy hospital once came to me to work on her own stress and self-care. In the session, I taught her the three-minute breathing space (Williams, Teasdale, Segal, & Kabat-Zinn, 2007), and she seemed to appreciate that it could be helpful for checking in with herself. When I suggested she practice it in the middle of the workday, she was very resistant, for a couple of reasons. For one thing, she felt that she was so busy at work that she did not have even 3 minutes to stop and check in, which is sadly a commonplace sentiment.

However, she also had a deeper concern. She was worried that if she stopped and sat still for 3 minutes, she would become relaxed and lose her motivation to do her work. At some level, she thought that her stress energized her to get things done faster, and if she lost that "edge," she would become unproductive.

Rather than trying to talk her into doing it, I simply said, "Well, we know that what you are doing now is not working for you, and definitely not sustainable in the long run. If you want a different outcome, you are going to have to do something different. Why don't you do it near the end of the workday? The worst that can happen is that you lose a little productivity at the end of the day."

Of course, pausing a few times a day does not radically change everything at first. But over time, she found that she was more present with her clients, and therefore able to more efficiently gather her assessment data. When she was writing a report, she was just writing that report and not thinking of the dozen other reports that were overdue. It turned out that her stress and her attempts to make efforts were actually interfering with her productivity.

Ultimately, since organizations are composed of people, and people can benefit from mindfulness training, it makes sense to continue promoting mindfulness in work settings (Badham & King, 2019). Asking people to ignore their distress and fake their emotions on a continuous basis is not a sustainable goal.

Summary: In general, studies of mindfulness in the workplace show a number of benefits to employees and thereby to the organizations for which they work. Of course, employers must be sensitive in adapting mindfulness programs to the particular needs of individual employees, and no one should be forced to do formal mindfulness practices.

Further Resources

Badham, R., & King, E. (2019). Mindfulness at work: A critical re-view. *Organization*, 1350508419888897.

Hafenbrack, A. C., & Vohs, K. D. (2018). Mindfulness meditation impairs task motivation but not performance. *Organizational Behavior and Human Decision Processes, 147*, 1–15.

Johnson, K. R., Park, S., & Chaudhuri, S. (2020). Mindfulness training in the workplace: Exploring its scope and outcomes. *European Journal of Training and Development, 44* (4/5), 341–354. https://doi.org/10.1108/EJTD-09 -2019-0156

Lyddy, C., Good, D. J., Bolino, M. C., Thompson, P. S., & Stephens, J. P. (2021). Where mindfulness falls short. *Harvard Business Review.* https://hbr .org/2021/03/where-mindfulness-falls-short

Otto, S. C., Wahl, K. R., Lefort, C. C., & Frei, W. H. (2012). Exploring the impact of multitasking in the workplace. *Journal of Business Studies Quarterly, 3*(4), 154.

Vonderlin, R., Biermann, M., Bohus, M., & Lyssenko, L. (2020). Mindfulness-based programs in the workplace: A meta-analysis of randomized controlled trials. *Mindfulness, 11*(7), 1579–1598.

Walsh, M. M., & Arnold, K. A. (2020). The bright and dark sides of employee mindfulness: Leadership style and employee well-being. *Stress and Health, 36*(3), 287–298.

Williams, M., Teasdale, J. D., Segal, Z. V., & Kabat-Zinn, J. (2007). *The mindful way through depression: Freeing yourself from chronic unhappiness.* Guilford Press.

Myth: I don't have time to be mindful. While many people agree that mindfulness could be helpful in their lives, it sounds to them like another chore, like making time to go to the gym for exercise. It sounds like just "one more thing" to have to add to their already busy lives.

Basis in truth: For many people, their lives are already packed with work, childcare, and household chores, so the thought of taking on another thing can seem daunting. No one wants a stress reduction program that adds stress to their lives. Beginning the formal practice of mindfulness does in fact take some time and effort.

Formal mindfulness programs, like MBSR (Kabat-Zinn, 2013) and MBCT (Segal, Williams, & Teasdale, 2013), typically have eight sessions, held once a week, with about an hour of homework practice each night. Such programs are designed to be a type of "boot camp" for kick starting the practice of mindfulness, and hence do require a commitment of time and energy.

Reality: Even if you are interested in a formal mindfulness program, but are very busy, all of us have 168 hours every week. We simply choose how we want to spend our time. For example, no one ever tells me they are too busy to brush their teeth or take a shower. We make time for the things that are important to us. Isn't it sad how often people do not make time for their own self-care? Of course, I never try to talk anyone into formal mindfulness practices. They are not for everyone.

While formal mindfulness exercises require you to set time aside for practice, and can be very helpful to get started, you can practice mindfulness even in the midst of a busy day. When you are cooking dinner, instead of ruminating about work or worrying about your retirement, you can just smell the food cooking. When you are walking around in your home or office, you can notice the people around you. When you are taking care of your children, you can look into their eyes and appreciate that they will only be this age once.

In any case, consider that time is an artificial measure. Clocks are very convenient for social conventions, like coordinating when to meet a friend for lunch, but time does not really "pass" like the ticking of clock. You are always in the present moment.

When I first started practicing mindfulness as a teenager, I tried sitting in front of a clock. I thought that if I could be fully present in the moment, I could get the second hand to stop. It never worked! Ticking is simply what clocks do. Seconds are useful measures but do not confuse them with the present moment (Sears, 2014).

The late philosopher Alan Watts (1971, 2003) warned people not to confuse the present moment with a split second. He called it the "eternal now," which is roomy and rich. In our minds, we think that the past goes back forever, the future goes forward forever, and the present is only a tiny hairline that connects them. However, when you practice mindfulness, you discover that the opposite is true. The past and future exist only in memory and thought, and you can only perceive through your senses right now.

Of course, we have real and practical issues to deal with in our daily lives, but if we carry those around in our heads all day, we will always feel busy. Consider this: *The feeling of busyness only comes when you are thinking about what you are not doing.*

For example, if you wake up first thing in the morning and look at your planner, you may see that you have a lot of chores, meetings, childcare, and countless other things on your to-do list. If you think about all those tasks all day long, you will feel busy. But the reality is, in that moment, you are only looking at your planner. All those other tasks are only in your mind. You can only do one thing at time. You put your planner down, you walk to the bathroom, you make your coffee, you sit down to reply to emails. You can be mindful in each of those activities. Yes, it is important to check your list from time to time and to prioritize which is most important, but the reality is you can only do one thing at a time, and constantly thinking about all those other things will only create stress.

There is only this moment. How can you say you do not have time to be in it? Only you can choose what to do with this present.

Summary: Formal mindfulness programs do require a time commitment, and it can be challenging for people to prioritize their own self-care. However, we are always in this moment, whether or not we choose to be in touch with our experiences. We can be mindful anytime we choose to be.

Further Resources

Kabat-Zinn, J. (2013). *Full catastrophe living: Using the wisdom of your body and mind to face stress, pain, and illness*, revised edition. Delta.

Sears, R. (2014). *Mindfulness: Living through challenges and enriching your life in this moment.* London, UK: Wiley-Blackwell.

Segal, Z., Williams, M., & Teasdale, J. (2013). *Mindfulness-based cognitive therapy for depression*, 2nd edition. New York: Guilford Press.

Watts, A. W. (2003). *Become what you are: Expanded edition.* Shambhala Publications.

References

Ader, R., & Cohen, N. (1975). Behaviorally conditioned immunosuppression. *Psychosomatic Medicine, 37*(4), 333–340.

Adler, R. F., & Benbunan-Fich, R. (2012). Juggling on a high wire: Multitasking effects on performance. *International Journal of Human-Computer Studies, 70*(2), 156–168.

Alkoby, A., Pliskin, R., Halperin, E., & Levit-Binnun, N. (2019). An eight-week mindfulness-based stress reduction (MBSR) workshop increases regulatory choice flexibility. *Emotion, 19*(4), 593.

American Psychological Association. (2014). Stress in America: Are teens adopting adults' stress habits? stress in America™ survey. Retrieved from https://www.apa.org/news/press/releases/stress/2013/stress-report.pdf

An, T. T. (1975). *Zen philosophy, Zen practice.* Dharma Publishing.

Azam, M. A., Latman, V. V., & Katz, J. (2019). Effects of a 12-minute smartphone-based mindful breathing task on heart rate variability for students with clinically relevant chronic pain, depression, and anxiety: Protocol for a randomized controlled trial. *JMIR Research Protocols, 8*(12), e14119.

Bach, P., & Moran, D. J. (2008). *ACT in practice: Case conceptualization in acceptance and commitment therapy.* Oakland, CA: New Harbinger Publications.

Badham, R., & King, E. (2019). Mindfulness at work: A critical re-view. *Organization,* 1350508419888897.

Baer, R. A. (Ed.). (2015). *Mindfulness-based treatment approaches: Clinician's guide to evidence base and applications.* Elsevier.

Barkley, R. A., & Benton, C. M. (2013). *Your defiant child: Eight steps to better behavior.* Guilford Press.

Basso, J. C., McHale, A., Ende, V., Oberlin, D. J., & Suzuki, W. A. (2019). Brief, daily meditation enhances attention, memory, mood, and emotional regulation in non-experienced meditators. *Behavioural Brain Research, 356,* 208–220.

Batchelor, S. (1987). *The jewel in the lotus: A guide to the Buddhist traditions of Tibet.* Wisdom Publications.

Bawa, F. L. M., Mercer, S. W., Atherton, R. J., Clague, F., Keen, A., Scott, N. W., & Bond, C. M. (2015). Does mindfulness improve outcomes in patients with chronic pain? Systematic review and meta-analysis. *British Journal of General Practice, 65*(635), e387–e400.

Beckman, H. B., Markakis, K. M., Suchman, A. L., & Frankel, R. M. (1994). The doctor-patient relationship and malpractice: Lessons from plaintiff depositions. *Archives of Internal Medicine, 154*(12), 1365–70.

Benson, H., & Klipper, M. Z. (2009). *The relaxation response.* New York: Morrow.

Berghoff, C. R., Wheeless, L. E., Ritzert, T. R., Wooley, C. M., & Forsyth, J. P. (2017). Mindfulness meditation adherence in a college sample: Comparison of a 10-min versus 20-min 2-week daily practice. *Mindfulness, 8*(6), 1513–1521.

Birnie, K., Speca, M., & Carlson, L. E. (2010). Exploring self-compassion and empathy in the context of mindfulness-based stress reduction (MBSR). *Stress and Health, 26,* 359–371.

Black, D. S., & Slavich, G. M. (2016). Mindfulness meditation and the immune system: A systematic review of randomized controlled trials. *Annals of the New York Academy of Sciences, 1373*(1), 13.

Blanck, P., Perleth, S., Heidenreich, T., Kröger, P., Ditzen, B., Bents, H., & Mander, J. (2018). Effects of mindfulness exercises as stand-alone intervention on symptoms of anxiety and depression: Systematic review and meta-analysis. *Behaviour Research and Therapy, 102,* 25–35.

Blofeld, J. (1978). *Taoism—The road to immortality.* Shambhala Publications.

Boccio, F. J. (1993). *Mindfulness yoga: The awakened union of breath, body, and mind.* Simon and Schuster.

Bohlmeijer, E., Prenger, R., Taal, E., & Cuijpers, P. (2010). The effects of mindfulness-based stress reduction therapy on mental health of adults with a chronic medical disease: A meta-analysis. *Journal of Psychosomatic Research, 68*(6), 539–544.

Bowen, S., Chawla, N., Grow, J., & Marlatt, G. A. (2021). *Mindfulness-based relapse prevention for addictive behaviors: A clinician's guide,* 2nd ed. New York: Guilford Press.

Brach, T. (2004). *Radical acceptance: Embracing your life with the heart of a Buddha.* Bantam Books.

Britton, W. B. (2019). Can mindfulness be too much of a good thing? The value of a middle way. *Current Opinion in Psychology, 28,* 159–165.

Bronkhorst, J. (1986). *The two traditions of meditation in ancient India.* Stuttgart: Franz Steiner.

Broughton, J. L., & Watanabe, E. Y. (2017). *The letters of Chan Master Dahui Pujue.* Oxford University Press.

Brown, D. P., & Engler, J. (1980). The stages of mindfulness meditation: A validation study. *The Journal of Transpersonal Psychology, 12*(2), 143.

Buddhadasa Bhikkhu (1996). *Mindfulness with breathing: A manual for serious beginners.* Wisdom Publications.

Burns, D. D., & Beck, A. T. (1999). *Feeling good: The new mood therapy.* Harper Publications.

Buswell Jr, R. E. (1991). *Tracing back the radiance: Chinul's Korean way of Zen.* University of Hawaii Press.

Byerly-Lamm, K. R. (2017). *The impact of mindfulness-based cognitive therapy (MBCT) on stress and affect in a community wellness group sample.* Doctoral dissertation, Union Institute and University.

Byrne, R. (2008). *The secret.* Simon and Schuster.

Carlson, N. R., & Birkett, M. A. (2021). *Physiology of behavior,* 13th edition. Pearson.

Carson, J. W., Carson, K. M., Gil, K. M., & Baucom, D. H. (2004). Mindfulness-based relationship enhancement. *Behavior Therapy, 35*(3), 471–494.

Chalmers, D. (2018). The meta-problem of consciousness. *Journal of Consciousness Studies, 25*(9–10), 6–61.

Chodron, P. (2001). *Start where you are: A guide to compassionate living.* Shambhala Publications.

Clair, E. S. (2016). *Bringing mindfulness and Brother Lawrence together: Christian implications for the modern Christian.* Doctoral Dissertation, Biola University.

Clark, W. R. (1998). *Sex and the origins of death.* Oxford University Press.

Cotton, C., Kraemer, K. M., Sears, R. W., Strawn, J. R., Wasson, R. S., Welge, J., Blom, T. J., Durling, M., & DelBello, M. P. (2019). Mindfulness-based cognitive therapy for children and adolescents with anxiety disorders at-risk for bipolar disorder: A psychoeducation waitlist controlled pilot trial. *Early Intervention in Psychiatry* (pp. 1–9). Doi: 10.1111/eip.12848

Cotton, S., Luberto, C., Sears, R. W., Strawn, J., Wasson, R., & DelBello, M. (2015). Mindfulness-based cognitive therapy for youth with anxiety disorders at risk for bipolar disorder: A pilot trial. *Early Intervention in Psychiatry.* Doi: 10.1111/eip.12216.

Crick, F., & Koch, C. (2003). A framework for consciousness. *Nature Neuroscience, 6*(2), 119–126.

Csikszentmihalyi, M. (1990). *Flow: The psychology of optimal experience*. New York: Harper & Row.

D'Aquili, E. G., & Newberg, A. B. (1999). *The mystical mind: Probing the biology of religious experience*. Minneapolis, MN: Fortress Press.

Dahl, J., & Lundgren, T. (2006). *Living beyond your pain: Using acceptance & commitment therapy to ease chronic pain*. New Harbinger.

Dalai Lama, & Cutler, H. C. (1998). *The art of happiness: A handbook for living*. Hodder & Stoughton, London.

Dalai Lama, & Ekman, P. (2008). *Emotional awareness: Overcoming the obstacles to psychological balance and compassion*. Macmillan.

Dalai Lama, Tsong-ka-pa, & Hopkins, J. (1987). *Tantra in Tibet: The great exposition of secret mantra*, Vol. 1. Snow Lion Publications.

Damasio, A. R. (2006). *Descartes' error*. Random House.

Das, L. S. (1998). *Awakening the Buddha within: Eight steps to enlightenment: Tibetan wisdom for the Western world*. Harmony.

Dass, R. (2010). *Be here now*. Harmony.

Davis, D., & Hayes, H. (2011). What are the benefits of mindfulness? A practice review of psychotherapy related research. *Psychotherapy*, *48*(2), 198–208. Doi: 10.1037/a0022062.

De Bloom, J., Geurts, S. A., & Kompier, M. A. (2013). Vacation (after-) effects on employee health and well-being, and the role of vacation activities, experiences and sleep. *Journal of Happiness Studies*, *14*(2), 613–633.

De Bloom, J., Kompier, M., Geurts, S., De Weerth, C., Taris, T., & Sonnentag, S. (2008). Do we recover from vacation? Meta-analysis of vacation effects on health and well-being. *Journal of Occupational Health*, 0812090045-0812090045.

de Vibe, M., Bjørndal, A., Fattah, S., Dyrdal, G. M., Halland, E., & Tanner-Smith, E. E. (2017). Mindfulness-based stress reduction (MBSR) for improving health, quality of life and social functioning in adults: A systematic review and meta-analysis. *Campbell Systematic Reviews*, *13*(1), 1–264.

Domjan, M. (2008). *The essentials of conditioning and learning*, 3rd ed. Belmont, CA: Wadsworth.

Dreyfus, G. (2011). Is mindfulness present-centred and non-judgmental? A discussion of the cognitive dimensions of mindfulness. *Contemporary Buddhism*, *12*(1), 41–54.

Drissi, I., Woods, W. A., & Woods, C. G. (2020). Understanding the genetic basis of congenital insensitivity to pain. *British Medical Bulletin*, *133*(1), 65.

Duggal, K. S. (1988). *Philosophy and faith of Sikhism*. Himalayan Institute Press.

Duncan, L., & Bardacke, N. (2010). Mindfulness-based childbirth and parenting education: Promoting family mindfulness during the perinatal period. *Journal of Child & Family Studies, 19*, 190–202. Doi: 10.1007/s10826-009-9313-7.

Emmons, R. A. (2007). *Thanks!: How the new science of gratitude can make you happier.* Houghton Mifflin Harcourt.

Emmons, R. A. (2008). Gratitude, subjective well-being, and the brain. *The Science of Subjective Well-Being,* 469–489.

Engeser, S., Schiepe-Tiska, A., & Peifer, C. (2021). Historical lines and an overview of current research on flow. *Advances in Flow Research,* 1–29.

Epel, E., Daubenmier, J., Moskowitz, J. T., Folkman, S., & Blackburn, E. (2009). Can meditation slow rate of cellular aging? Cognitive stress, mindfulness, and telomeres. *Annals of the New York Academy of Sciences, 1172,* 34.

Epstein, D. E. (2017). The role of home practice engagement in a Mindfulness-Based Intervention [ProQuest Information & Learning]. In *Dissertation Abstracts International: Section B: The Sciences and Engineering* (Vol. 77, Issue 9–B(E)).

Epstein, M. (2009). *Going on being: Life at the crossroads of Buddhism and psychotherapy.* Simon and Schuster.

Etzel, L. C., & Shalev, I. (2021). Effects of psychological stress on telomeres as genome regulators. In G. Fink (Ed.), *Stress: Genetics, epigenetics and genomics* (pp. 109–117). Academic Press.

Frankl, V. E. (1985). *Man's search for meaning.* Simon and Schuster.

Fulton, P. (2005). Mindfulness as clinical training. In C. Germer, R. Siegel, & P. Fulton (Eds.), *Mindfulness and psychotherapy* (pp. 55–72). New York: Guilford Press.

Gafner, G., & Benson, S. (2003). *Hypnotic techniques: For standard psychotherapy and formal hypnosis.* WW Norton & Co.

Germer, C. (2009). *The mindful path to self-compassion: Freeing yourself from destructive thoughts and emotions.* Guilford Press.

Giannandrea, A., Simione, L., Pescatori, B., Ferrell, K., Belardinelli, M. O., Hickman, S. D., & Raffone, A. (2019). Effects of the mindfulness-based stress reduction program on mind wandering and dispositional mindfulness facets. *Mindfulness, 10*(1), 185–195.

Goldberg, S. B., Del Re, A. C., Hoyt, W. T., & Davis, J. M. (2014). The secret ingredient in mindfulness interventions? A case for practice quality over quantity. *Journal of Counseling Psychology, 61*(3), 491.

Goleman, D., & Davidson, R. J. (2017). *Altered traits: Science reveals how meditation changes your mind, brain, and body.* Penguin Books.

Gotink, R. A., Chu, P., Busschbach, J. J., Benson, H., Fricchione, G. L., & Hunink, M. M. (2015). Standardised mindfulness-based interventions in healthcare: An overview of systematic reviews and meta-analyses of RCTs. *PloS One, 10*(4), e0124344.

Greenberg, M. T., & Harris, A. R. (2012). Nurturing mindfulness in children and youth: Current state of research. *Child Development Perspectives, 6*(2), 161–166.

Greenberger, D., & Padesky, C. A. (2015). *Mind over mood: Change how you feel by changing the way you think.* Guilford Publications.

Grepmair, L., Mietterlehner, F., Loew, T., Bachler, E., Rother, W., & Nickel, N. (2007). Promoting mindfulness in psychotherapists in training influences the treatment results of their patients: A randomized, double-blind, controlled study. *Psychotherapy and Psychosomatics, 76,* 332–338. Doi: 10.1159/000107560.

Grossman, P., Niemann, L., Schmidt, S., & Walach, H. (2004). Mindfulness-based stress reduction and health benefits: A meta-analysis. *Journal of Psychosomatic Research, 57*(1), 35–43.

Gul, L., & Jahangir, S. F. (2019). The Effectiveness of Mindfulness-Based Stress Reduction Programme (MBSRP) and Sufi Meditation (SM) in the Treatment of Neurotic Anxiety among Females. *FWU Journal of Social Sciences, 13*(1), 120–130.

Gunaratana, B. H. (1996). *Mindfulness in plain English, revised and expanded edition.* Wisdom Publications.

Gunaratana, H. (2012). *The four foundations of mindfulness in plain English.* Simon and Schuster.

Gür, G. C., & Yilmaz, E. (2020). The effects of mindfulness-based empathy training on empathy and aged discrimination in nursing students: A randomised controlled trial. *Complementary Therapies in Clinical Practice, 39,* 101140.

Hafenbrack, A. C., & Vohs, K. D. (2018). Mindfulness meditation impairs task motivation but not performance. *Organizational Behavior and Human Decision Processes, 147,* 1–15.

Hahn, T. N., & Anh-Huong, N. (2019). *Walking meditation: Easy steps to mindfulness.* Sounds True.

Hameroff, S. R., & Penrose, R. (2017). Consciousness in the universe: An updated review of the "ORCH OR" theory. In R. Poznanski, J. Tuszynski, & T. Feinberg (Eds.), *Biophysics of consciousness: A foundational approach* (pp. 517–599). World Scientific.

Hanh, T. N. (2008). *The miracle of mindfulness: The classic guide to meditation by the world's most revered master.* London: Rider.

Hanson, R., & Mendius, R. (2009). *Buddha's brain: The practical neuroscience of happiness, love & wisdom.* Oakland, CA: New Harbinger Publications.

Harris, R. (2008). *The happiness trap: How to stop struggling and start living.* Trumpeter.

Harris, R. (2009). Mindfulness without meditation. *Healthcare Counselling and Psychotherapy Journal, 9*(4), 21–24.

Harrison, P. (2014). *The mindfulness movie* [DVD]. Where's My Mind? Media.

Hart, W., & Goenka, S. N. (2019). *The art of living: Vipassana meditation as taught by SN Goenka.* Embassy Books.

Hartranft, C. (2003). *The Yoga-Sutra of Patanjali: A new translation with commentary.* Shambhala Publications.

Hayes, S. C. (2005). *Get out of your mind and into your life: The new acceptance and commitment therapy.* New Harbinger Publications.

Hayes, S. C. (2020a). *A liberated mind: How to pivot toward what matters.* Avery.

Hayes, S. C. (2020b). *ACT Immersion: An introduction to ACT as a process-based therapy* [Online Video Course]. Retrieved from https://act.courses/signup/

Hayes, S. C., & Hofmann, S. G. (Eds.). (2018). *Process-based CBT: The science and core clinical competencies of cognitive behavioral therapy.* New Harbinger Publications.

Hayes, S. C., Strosahl, K., & Wilson, K. G. (2012). *Acceptance and commitment therapy: The process and practice of mindful change*, 2nd ed. New York: Guilford Press.

Hayes, S. K. (2012). *The Ninja defense: A modern master's approach to universal dangers.* Tuttle Publishing.

Hayes, S. K. (2013). *The complete ninja collection.* Black Belt Communications.

Hayes, S. K. (2019). *Action meditation: The Japanese diamond and lotus tradition.* Nine Gates Press.

Hebb, D. O. (1949). *The organization of behavior.* New York: Wiley & Sons.

Helminski, K. E. (2017). *Living presence (revised): The Sufi path to mindfulness and the essential self.* Penguin.

Hente, E., Sears, R., Cotton, S., Pallerla, H., Siracusa, C., Spear Filigno, S., & Boat, T. (2020). Mindfulness-based cognitive therapy to reduce stress and improve well-being for health professionals providing chronic disease care. *Journal of Pediatrics*, May. Doi: 10.1016/j.jpeds.2020.02.081

Hick, S. F., & Bien, T. (2008). *Mindfulness and the therapeutic relationship.* New York, NY: Guilford Press.

Hilton, L., Hempel, S., Ewing, B. A., Apaydin, E., Xenakis, L., Newberry, S., … & Maglione, M. A. (2017). Mindfulness meditation for chronic pain:

Systematic review and meta-analysis. *Annals of Behavioral Medicine, 51*(2), 199–213.

Hirai, T. (1989). *Zen meditation and psychotherapy.* New York: Japan Publications.

Hitchcock, P. F., Martin, L. M., Fischer, L., Marando-Blanck, S., & Herbert, J. D. (2016). Popular conceptions of mindfulness: Awareness and emotional control. *Mindfulness, 7*(4), 940–949.

Hofmann, S. G., Grossman, P., & Hinton, D. E. (2011). Loving-kindness and compassion meditation: Potential for psychological interventions. *Clinical Psychology Review, 31*(7), 1126–1132.

Hollis-Walker, L., & Colosimo, K. (2011). Mindfulness, self-compassion, and happiness in non-meditators: A theoretical and empirical examination. *Personality and Individual Differences, 50,* 222–227.

Hölzel, B., Lazar, S., Gard, T., Schuman-Olivier, Z., Vago, D., & Ott, U. (2011). How does mindfulness meditation work? Proposing mechanisms of action from a conceptual and neural perspective. *Perspectives on Psychological Science, 6*(6) 537–559. Doi: 10.1177/1745691611419671.

Hopkins, J. (1992). *Walking through walls: A presentation of Tibetan meditation.* Snow Lion Publications.

Huntington, B., & Kuhn, N. (2003). Communication gaffes: A root cause of malpractice claims. *Proceedings, Baylor University Medical Center, 16*(2), 157–161.

Hyland, T. (2015). McMindfulness in the workplace: Vocational learning and the commodification of the present moment. *Journal of Vocational Education & Training, 67*(2), 219–234.

Intarakamhang, U., Macaskill, A., & Prasittichok, P. (2020). Mindfulness interventions reduce blood pressure in patients with non-communicable diseases: A systematic review and meta-analysis. *Heliyon, 6*(4), e03834.

Ijaz, S., Khalily, M. T., & Ahmad, I. (2017). Mindfulness in salah prayer and its association with mental health. *Journal of Religion and Health, 56*(6), 2297–2307.

Irving, J. A., Dobkin, P. L., & Park, J. (2009). Cultivating mindfulness in health care professionals: A review of empirical studies of mindfulness-based stress reduction (MBSR). *Complementary Therapies in Clinical Practice, 15*(2), 61–66.

Isgandarova, N. (2019). Muraqaba as a mindfulness-based therapy in Islamic psychotherapy. *Journal of Religion and Health, 58*(4), 1146–1160.

Isis, P. (2016). *The mindful doodle book: Seventy-five creative exercises to help you live in the moment.* PESI Publishing and Media.

Ison, D. C. (2015). Comparative analysis of accident and non-accident pilots. *Journal of Aviation Technology and Engineering, 4*(2–2). Doi: 10.7771/2159-6670.1103

Jacobson, E. (1934). *You must relax.* Whittlesey House.

Jacobson, E. (1938). Progressive muscle relaxation. *Journal of Abnormal Psychology, 75*(1), 18.

Jha, A. P., Krompinger, J., & Baime, M. J. (2007). Mindfulness training modifies subsystems of attention. *Cognitive, Affective, & Behavioral Neuroscience, 7*(2), 109–119.

Johnson, K. R., Park, S., & Chaudhuri, S. (2020). Mindfulness training in the workplace: Exploring its scope and outcomes. *European Journal of Training and Development, 44*(4/5), 341–354. Doi: 10.1108/EJTD-09-2019-0156

Jones, S. M., Bodie, G. D., & Hughes, S. D. (2019). The impact of mindfulness on empathy, active listening, and perceived provisions of emotional support. *Communication Research, 46*(6), 838–865.

Kabat-Zinn, J. (2003). Mindfulness-based interventions in context: Past, present, and future. *Clinical Psychology: Science and Practice, 10*(2), 144–156.

Kabat-Zinn, J. (2005). *Coming to our senses: Healing ourselves and the world through mindfulness.* Hachette UK.

Kabat-Zinn, J. (2009). *Wherever you go, there you are: Mindfulness meditation in everyday life.* Hachette Books.

Kabat-Zinn, J. (2010). *Mindfulness meditation for pain relief: Guided practices for reclaiming your body and your life* [audio CD]. Boulder, CO: Sounds True.

Kabat-Zinn, J. (2013). *Full catastrophe living: Using the wisdom of your body and mind to face stress, pain, and illness,* revised edition. Delta.

Kabat-Zinn, J. (2021). *Guided mindfulness meditations: Series 1* [audio recording]. Mindfulnesscds.com.

Kelly, L. (2019). *The way of effortless mindfulness: A revolutionary guide for living an awakened life.* Sounds True.

Kemper, K. J., & Khirallah, M. (2015). Acute effects of online mind–body skills training on resilience, mindfulness, and empathy. *Journal of Evidence-Based Complementary & Alternative Medicine, 20*(4), 247–253.

Khalsa, D. S., Amen, D., Hanks, C., Money, N., & Newberg, A. (2009). Cerebral blood flow changes during chanting meditation. *Nuclear Medicine Communications, 30*(12), 956–961.

Khoury, B., Lecomte, T., Gaudiano, B. A., & Paquin, K. (2013). Mindfulness interventions for psychosis: A meta-analysis. *Schizophrenia Research, 150*(1), 176–184.

Kilpatrick, L. A., Suyenobu, B. Y., Smith, S. R., Bueller, J. A., Goodman, T., Creswell, J. D., ... & Naliboff, B. D. (2011). Impact of mindfulness-based stress reduction training on intrinsic brain connectivity. *Neuroimage, 56*(1), 290–298.

Kingsbury, E. (2009). *The relationship between empathy and mindfulness: Understanding the role of self-compassion.* ProQuest Information & Learning.

Kinomura, S., Larsson, J., Gulyas, B., & Roland, P. E. (1996). Activation by attention of the human reticular formation and thalamic intralaminar nuclei. *Science, 271*(5248), 512–515. Doi: 10.1126/science.271.5248.512

Kirsch, I., & Braffman, W. (2001). Imaginative suggestibility and hypnotizability. *Current Directions in Psychological Science, 10*(2), 57–61.

Klayman, J. (1995). Varieties of confirmation bias. *Psychology of Learning and Motivation, 32,* 385–418.

Kok, B. E., Coffey, K. A., Cohn, M. A., Catalino, L. I., Vacharkulksemsuk, T., Algoe, S. B., ... & Fredrickson, B. L. (2013). How positive emotions build physical health: Perceived positive social connections account for the upward spiral between positive emotions and vagal tone. *Psychological Science, 24*(7), 1123–1132.

Kornfield, J. (2006). *Mindfulness, bliss, and beyond: A meditator's handbook.* Simon and Schuster.

Kostanski, M., & Hassed, C. (2008). Mindfulness as a concept and a process. *Australian Psychologist, 43*(1), 15–21.

Kraemer, K. M., Wasson, R., Lyle, K., Wu, G., Sears, R., Attari, M., & Cotton, S. (2015, October). *A four session mindfulness program for improving stress and well-being among college of medicine faculty.* Poster presentation at CENTILE International Conference to Promote Resilience, Empathy and Well-Being in Health Care Professions, Washington, DC.

Krishnamurti, J. (2000). *Choiceless awareness: A selection of passages for the study of the teachings of J. Krishnamurti.* Krishnamurti Foundation of America.

Kristeller, J., & Bowman, A. (2015). *The joy of half a cookie: Using mindfulness to lose weight and end the struggle with food.* New York: Perigee.

Kristeller, J., & Wolever, R. (2011). Mindfulness-based eating awareness training for treating binge eating disorder: The conceptual foundation. *Eating Disorders, 19*(1), 49–61. Doi: 10.1080/10640266.2011.533605.

Kumat, R. S. (2007). *Self awareness through meditation: A comparative study of Jain, Buddha, Yoga Darshanas and modern thinkers.* Xlibris.

Kuyken, W., Watkins, E., Holden, E., White, K., Taylor, R. S., Byford, S., ... Dalgleish, T. (2010). How does mindfulness-based cognitive therapy work? *Behaviour Research and Therapy, 48*(11), 1105–1112.

Lazar, S. W., Kerr, C. E., Wasserman, R. H., Gray, J. R., Greve, D. N., Treadway, M. T., … Fischl, B. (2005). Meditation experience is associated with increased cortical thickness. *Neuroreport, 16*(17), 1893–1897.

Laird, M. (2006). *Into the silent land: A guide to the Christian practice of contemplation*. Oxford University Press.

Leahy, R. L., Tirch, D., & Napolitano, L. A. (2011). *Emotion regulation in psychotherapy: A practitioner's guide*. Guilford Press.

Ledesma, D., & Kumano, H. (2009). Mindfulness-based stress reduction and cancer: A meta-analysis. *Psycho-Oncology: Journal of the Psychological, Social and Behavioral Dimensions of Cancer, 18*(6), 571–579.

Lester, G. W. (2018). *Advanced diagnosis, treatment, and management of DSM-5 personality disorders*. Eau Claire, WI: PESI.

Lester, E. G., & Murrell, A. R. (2019). Becoming mindful of measurement: An experimental-experiential analogue study of state mindfulness measures. *Mindfulness, 10*(10), 2133–2142.

Lester, E. G., Murrell, A. R., & Dickson, D. E. (2018). A mixed methods approach to understanding conceptions of mindfulness meditation. *OBM Integrative and Complementary Medicine, 3*(4), 026.

Libet, B., Gleason, C. A., Wright, Jr, E. W., & Pearl, D. K. (1983). Time of conscious intention to act in relation to onset of cerebral activity (readiness-potential). *Brain, 106*, 623–642.

Linehan, M. (2015a). *DBT skills training handouts and worksheets*. New York: Guilford Press.

Linehan, M. (2015b). *Skills training manual for treating borderline personality disorder*, 2nd ed. New York: Guilford Press.

Linehan, M. M. (2020). *Dialectical behavior therapy in clinical practice*. Guilford Publications.

Lloyd, A., White, R., Eames, C., & Crane, R. (2018). The utility of home-practice in mindfulness-based group interventions: A systematic review. *Mindfulness, 9*(3), 673–692.

Longmore, R., & Worrell, M. (2007). Do we need to challenge thoughts in cognitive behavior therapy? *Clinical Psychology Review, 27*, 173–187.

Lovas, D. A., & Schuman-Olivier, Z. (2018). Mindfulness-based cognitive therapy for bipolar disorder: A systematic review. *Journal of Affective Disorders, 240*, 247–261.

Luberto, C. M., Hall, D. L., Park, E. R., Haramati, A., & Cotton, S. (2020). A perspective on the similarities and differences between mindfulness and relaxation. *Global Advances in Health and Medicine, 9*, 2164956120905597.

Luberto, C. M., & McLeish, A. C. (2018). The effects of a brief mindfulness exercise on state mindfulness and affective outcomes among adult daily smokers. *Addictive Behaviors, 77*, 73–80.

Luberto, C. M., Wasson, R. S., Kraemer, K. M., Sears, R. W., Hueber, C., & Cotton, S. (2017). Feasibility, acceptability, and preliminary effectiveness of a 4-week Mindfulness-Based Cognitive Therapy protocol for hospital employees. *Mindfulness, 8*(6), 1522–1531. Doi: 10.1007/s12671-017-0718-x

Luberto, C. M., White, C., Sears, R. W., & Cotton, S. (2013). Integrative medicine for treating depression: An update on the latest evidence. *Current Psychiatry Reports, 15*(9), 391–393.

Ludwig, D. S., & Kabat-Zinn, J. (2008). Mindfulness in medicine. *JAMA, 300*(11), 1350–1352.

Luk, C. (1964). *The secrets of Chinese meditation.* Samuel Weiser.

Lush, P., & Dienes, Z. (2019). Time perception and the experience of agency in meditation and hypnosis. *PsyCh Journal, 8*(1), 36–50.

Lyddy, C., Good, D. J., Bolino, M. C., Thompson, P. S., & Stephens, J. P. (2021). Where mindfulness falls short. *Harvard Business Review.* Retrieved from https://hbr.org/2021/03/where-mindfulness-falls-short

Lymeus, F., Lundgren, T., & Hartig, T. (2017). Attentional effort of beginning mindfulness training is offset with practice directed toward images of natural scenery. *Environment and Behavior, 49*(5), 536–559.

McBee, L. (2008). *Mindfulness-based elder care: A CAM model for frail elders and their caregivers.* New York: Springer Pub.

McCullough, M. E., Tsang, J. A., & Emmons, R. A. (2004). Gratitude in intermediate affective terrain: Links of grateful moods to individual differences and daily emotional experience. *Journal of Personality and Social Psychology, 86*(2), 295.

McDonald, K. (2005). *How to meditate: A practical guide.* Simon and Schuster.

McKay, M., & Fanning, P. (2008). *Progressive relaxation and breathing: Relaxation & stress reduction audio series* [Audio CD]. New Harbinger.

McKay, T., & Walker, B. R. (2021). Mindfulness, self-compassion and wellbeing. *Personality and Individual Differences, 168,* 110412.

Mikulas, W. L. (2011). Mindfulness: Significant common confusions. *Mindfulness, 2*(1), 1–7.

Mikulas, W. L. (2015). Ethics in Buddhist training. *Mindfulness, 6*(1), 14–16.

Miller, L. D. (2014). *Effortless mindfulness: Genuine mental health through awakened presence.* Routledge.

Miltenberger, R. (2012). *Behavior modification, principles and procedures,* 5th ed. (pp. 87–99). Wadsworth Publishing Company.

Milton, I. (2011). What does mindfulness really mean?: Clarifying key terms and definitions-part I. *Psychotherapy in Australia, 17*(4), 78.

Moreau, V., Rouleau, N., & Morin, C. M. (2013). Sleep, attention, and executive functioning in children with attention-deficit/hyperactivity disorder. *Archives of Clinical Neuropsychology, 28*(7), 692–699.

National Sleep Foundation. (2021). How much sleep do we really need? Retrieved from http://www.sleepfoundation.org/article/how-sleep-works/how-much-sleep-do-we-really-need

Neff, K. D. (2003). Self-compassion: An alternative conceptualization of a healthy attitude toward oneself. *Self and Identity, 2*, 85–101.

Neff, K., & Germer, C. (2018). *The mindful self-compassion workbook: A proven way to accept yourself, build inner strength, and thrive.* Guilford Publications.

Nenadic, I., Güllmar, D., Dietzek, M., Langbein, K., Steinke, J., & Gaser, C. (2015). Brain structure in narcissistic personality disorder: A VBM and DTI pilot study. *Psychiatry Research: Neuroimaging, 231*(2), 184–186. Retrieved from https://doi-org.proxy.libraries.uc.edu/10.1016/j.pscychresns.2014.11.001

Newberg, A., d'Aquili, E. G., & Rause, V. (2008). *Why God won't go away: Brain science and the biology of belief.* Ballantine Books.

Nickerson, R. S. (1998). Confirmation bias: A ubiquitous phenomenon in many guises. *Review of General Psychology, 2*(2), 175–220.

Nisbet, E. K., Zelenski, J. M., & Grandpierre, Z. (2019). Mindfulness in nature enhances connectedness and mood. *Ecopsychology, 11*(2), 81–91.

Norris, C. J. (2021). The negativity bias, revisited: Evidence from neuroscience measures and an individual differences approach. *Social Neuroscience, 16*(1), 68–82.

O'Bryan, E., Kraemer, K., Luberto, C., & Sears, R. (2019). Mindfulness-based treatments for PTSD. In B. A. Moore & W. E. Penk (Eds.), *Treating PTSD in Military Personnel: A Clinical Handbook*, 2nd ed. New York, NY: Guilford Press.

O'Hare, D., Chalmers, D., & Scuffham, P. (2006). Case-control study of risk factors for fatal and non-fatal injury crashes of rotary-wing aircraft. *Journal of Safety Research, 37*(3), 293–298.

O'Neill, A., & Frodl, T. (2012). Brain structure and function in borderline personality disorder. *Brain Structure and Function, 217*(4), 767–782.

Otto, S. C., Wahl, K. R., Lefort, C. C., & Frei, W. H. (2012). Exploring the impact of multitasking in the workplace. *Journal of Business Studies Quarterly, 3*(4), 154.

Parsons, C. E., Crane, C., Parsons, L. J., Fjorback, L. O., & Kuyken, W. (2017). Home practice in mindfulness-based cognitive therapy and mindfulness-based stress reduction: A systematic review and meta-analysis of participants' mindfulness practice and its association with outcomes. *Behaviour Research and Therapy, 95*, 29–41.

Paulson, J., Huggins, V., & Gentile, D. A. (2019). Mindful awareness training: A pilot study integrating mindfulness practices into a rural jail-based substance abuse program. *Contemporary Rural Social Work Journal, 11*(1), 5.

Pavlov, I. P. (1927). *Conditioned reflexes: An investigation of the physiological activity of the cerebral cortex*, Trans. G. V. Anrep. New York: Dover.

Perlis, M. L, Jungquist, C., Smith, M. T., & Posner, D. (2008). *Cognitive behavioral treatment of insomnia: A session by session guide.* Springer.

Phelan, T. W. (2010). *1-2-3 Magic: Effective discipline for children 2–12.* ParentMagic, Inc.

Piaget, J. (1950). *The psychology of intelligence.* New York, NY: Harcourt Brace.

Piaget, J., & Morf, A. (1958). Les isomorphismes partiels entre les structures logiques et les structures perceptives. In J. Piaget (Ed.), *Etudes d'epistemologie genetique, Vol VI: Logique et perception* (pp. 52–166). Paris, France: Paris Presses Universitaires de France.

Posner, M. I., & Rafal, R. D. (1986). Cognitive theories of attention and the rehabilitation of attentional deficits. In M. J. Meier, A. L. Benton, & L. Miller (Eds.), *Neuropsychological rehabilitation* (pp. 182–201). New York: Guilford Press.

Purser, R. (2019). *McMindfulness: How mindfulness became the new capitalist spirituality.* Repeater.

Purser, R., & Loy, D. (2013). Beyond mcmindfulness. *Huffington Post, 1*(7), 13.

Quattrini, G., Pini, L., Pievani, M., Magni, L. R., Lanfredi, M., Ferrari, C., . . . Rossi, R. (2019). Abnormalities in functional connectivity in borderline personality disorder: Correlations with metacognition and emotion dysregulation. *Psychiatry Research: Neuroimaging, 283*, 118–124. Retrieved from https://doi-org.proxy.libraries.uc.edu/10.1016/j.pscychresns.2018.12.010

Querstret, D., Morison, L., Dickinson, S., Cropley, M., & John, M. (2020). Mindfulness-based stress reduction and mindfulness-based cognitive therapy for psychological health and well-being in nonclinical samples: A systematic review and meta-analysis. *International Journal of Stress Management, 27*(4), 394–411. Doi: 10.1037/str0000165

Rāhula, W. (1974). *What the Buddha taught.* Grove Press.

Raine, A., Meloy, J. R., Bihrle, S., Stoddard, J., et al. (1998). Reduced prefrontal and increased subcortical brain functioning assessed using positron emission tomography in predatory and affective murderers. *Behavioral Science and the Law, 16*, 319–332.

Raine, A., Lencz, T., Bihrle, S., LaCasse, L., et al. (2000). Reduced prefrontal gray matter volume and reduced autonomic activity in antisocial personality disorder. *Archives of General Psychiatry, 57*(2), 119–127.

Reddy, S. (2016). The best temperature for a good night's sleep: Light and time aren't as important as temperature, new research shows. *Wall Street Journal*, February 22.

Rescorla, R. A., & Heth, C. D. (1975). Reinstatement of fear to an extinguished conditioned stimulus. *Journal of Experimental Psychology: Animal Behavioral Processes, 1*(1), 88–96.

Ribeiro, L., Atchley, R. M., & Oken, B. S. (2018). Adherence to practice of mindfulness in novice meditators: Practices chosen, amount of time practiced, and long-term effects following a mindfulness-based intervention. *Mindfulness, 9*(2), 401–411.

Rosenbaum, R., & Magid, B. (Eds.). (2016). *What's wrong with mindfulness (and what isn't): Zen perspectives.* Simon and Schuster.

Rozin, P., & Royzman, E. B. (2001). Negativity bias, negativity dominance, and contagion. *Personality and Social Psychology Review, 5*(4), 296–320.

Saddhatissa, H. (1997). *Buddhist ethics.* Simon and Schuster.

Salmon, P., Lush, E., Jablonski, M., & Sephton, S. E. (2009). Yoga and mindfulness: Clinical aspects of an ancient mind/body practice. *Cognitive and Behavioral Practice, 16*(1), 59–72.

Salyers, C. (2017). Three insights from six reasons: Reflections on a Sufi mindfulness practice in performance. *Journal of Performance and Mindfulness, 1*(1), 1.

Salzberg, S. (2002). *Lovingkindness: The revolutionary art of happiness.* Shambhala Publications.

Salzberg, S. (2011). Mindfulness and loving-kindness. *Contemporary Buddhism, 12*(1), 177–182.

Sangara, T. (2017). *Spirituality and mindfulness in personal development and therapeutic practice.* Doctoral dissertation, City University of Seattle.

Sapolsky, R. M. (2004). *Why zebras don't get ulcers: The acclaimed guide to stress, stress-related diseases, and coping.* Holt paperbacks.

Schon, K. R., Parker, A. P. J., & Woods, C. G. (2020). Congenital insensitivity to pain overview. *GeneReviews® [Internet].*

Scott-Sheldon, L. A., Gathright, E. C., Donahue, M. L., Balletto, B., Feulner, M. M., DeCosta, J., … & Salmoirago-Blotcher, E. (2020). Mindfulness-based interventions for adults with cardiovascular disease: A systematic review and meta-analysis. *Annals of Behavioral Medicine, 54*(1), 67–73.

Sears, R. (2014). *Mindfulness: Living through challenges and enriching your life in this moment.* London, UK: Wiley-Blackwell.

Sears, R. (2017a). *The sense of self: Perspectives from science and Zen Buddhism.* New York: SpringerNature.

Sears, R. (2017b). *The cognitive-behavioral therapy and mindfulness toolbox.* Eau Claire, WI: PESI Publishing & Media, Inc.

Sears, R. (2021). *ACT with anxiety: An acceptance and commitment therapy workbook to get you unstuck from anxiety and enrich your life.* Eau Claire, WI: PESI Publishing & Media, Inc.

Sears, R. W., Bruns, K., Cotton, S., DelBello, M. P., Strawn, J. R., Kraemer, K., Wasson, R., Norris, M., Weber, W. A., & Durling, M. (2021, in preparation). *Neurofunctional changes associated with mindfulness-based cognitive therapy in mood dysregulated youth at risk for developing bipolar disorder.*

Sears, R., & Chard, K. (2016). *Mindfulness-based cognitive therapy for PTSD.* London, UK: Wiley-Blackwell.

Sears, R., Tirch, D., & Denton, R. B. (2011). *Mindfulness in clinical practice.* Sarasota, FL: Professional Resource Press.

Segal, Z., Williams, M., & Teasdale, J. (2013). *Mindfulness-based cognitive therapy for depression,* 2nd ed. New York: Guilford Press.

Semple, R., & Lee, J. (2011). *Mindfulness-based cognitive therapy for anxious children.* Oakland, CA: New Harbinger Publications, Inc.

Şenel, E. (2019). Dharmic religions and health: A holistic analysis of global health literature related to Hinduism, Buddhism, Sikhism and Jainism. *Journal of Religion and Health, 58*(4), 1161–1171.

Seung, Sahn (1997). *The compass of Zen.* Shambhala Publications.

Seung, Sahn (1999). *Only don't know: Selected teaching letters of Zen Master Seung Sahn.* Shambhala Publications.

Shapiro, S. L., Astin, J. A., Bishop, S. R., & Cordova, M. (2005). Mindfulness-based stress reduction for health care professionals: Results from a randomized trial. *International Journal of Stress Management, 12,* 164–176.

Shapiro, S., Brown, K., & Biegel, G. (2007). Teaching self-care to caregivers: Effects of mindfulness-based stress reduction on the mental health of therapists in training. *Training and Education in Professional Psychology, 1,* 105–115.

Shapiro, S., Siegel, R., & Neff, K. D. (2018). Paradoxes of mindfulness. *Mindfulness, 9*(6), 1693–1701.

Siegel, D. J. (2007). *The mindful brain: Reflection and attunement in the cultivation of well-being* (Norton series on interpersonal neurobiology). WW Norton & Company.

Siegel, R. D., Germer, C. K., & Olendzki, A. (2009). Mindfulness: What is it? where did it come from?. In: F. Didonna (Ed.), *Clinical handbook of mindfulness.* New York: Springer. Doi: 10.1007/978-0-387-09593-6_2

Sohlberg, M. M., & Mateer, C. A. (1989). *Introduction to cognitive rehabilitation: Theory and practice.* New York: Guilford Press.

Small, C., & Lew, C. (2019). Mindfulness, moral reasoning and responsibility: Towards virtue in ethical decision-making. *Journal of Business Ethics*, 1–15.

Smesny, S., Große, J., Gussew, A., Langbein, K., Schönfeld, N., Wagner, G., … Reichenbach, J. R. (2018). Prefrontal glutamatergic emotion regulation is disturbed in cluster B and C personality disorders—A combined ^{1}H/^{31}P-MR spectroscopic study. *Journal of Affective Disorders, 227*, 688–697. Retrieved from https://doi-org.proxy.libraries.uc.edu/10.1016/j.jad.2017.10.044

Smith, S. M., Fox, P. T., Miller, K. L., Glahn, D. C., Fox, P. M., Mackay, C. E., … & Beckmann, C. F. (2009). Correspondence of the brain's functional architecture during activation and rest. *Proceedings of the National Academy of Sciences, 106*(31), 13040–13045.

Sng, A. A., & Janca, A. (2016). Mindfulness for personality disorders. *Current Opinion in Psychiatry, 29*(1), 70–76.

Strawn, J., Cotton, S., Luberto, C., Patino, L., Stahl, L., Weber, W., Eliassen, J., Sears, R., & DelBello, M. (2016). Neurofunctional changes associated with mindfulness-based cognitive therapy in anxious youth at risk for developing bipolar disorder. *Journal of Child & Adolescent Psychopharmacology, 26*(4), 372–379. Doi: 10.1089/cap.2015.0054

Strohmaier, S., Jones, F. W., & Cane, J. E. (2021). Effects of length of mindfulness practice on mindfulness, depression, anxiety, and stress: A randomized controlled experiment. *Mindfulness, 12*(1), 198–214.

Stuart, D. M. (2017). Insight transformed: Coming to terms with mindfulness in South Asian and global frames. *Religions of South Asia, 11*(2–3), 158–181.

Suzuki, S. (2020). *Zen mind, beginner's mind.* Shambhala Publications.

Symington, S. H., & Symington, M. F. (2012). A Christian model of mindfulness: Using mindfulness principles to support psychological well-being, value-based behavior, and the Christian spiritual journey. *Journal of Psychology and Christianity, 31*(1), 71.

Tan, S. Y. (2011). Mindfulness and acceptance-based cognitive behavioral therapies: Empirical evidence and clinical applications from a Christian perspective. *Journal of Psychology and Christianity, 30*(3), 243.

Tang, Y. Y., Hölzel, B. K., & Posner, M. I. (2015). The neuroscience of mindfulness meditation. *Nature Reviews Neuroscience, 16*(4), 213–225.

Tang, Y. Y., & Posner, M. I. (2013). Tools of the trade: Theory and method in mindfulness neuroscience. *Social Cognitive and Affective Neuroscience, 8*(1), 118–120.

Teasdale, J., Williams, M., & Segal, Z. (2014). *The mindful way workbook: An 8-week program to free yourself from depression and emotional distress.* New York: Guilford Press.

Thomas, J., Furber, S. W., & Grey, I. (2017). The rise of mindfulness and its resonance with the Islamic tradition. *Mental Health, Religion & Culture, 20*(10), 973–985.

Tirch, D., Schoendorff, B., & Silberstein, L. R. (2014). *The ACT practitioner's guide to the science of compassion: Tools for fostering psychological flexibility.* New Harbinger Publications.

Tirch, D., Silberstein, L. R., & Kolts, R. L. (2015). *Buddhist psychology and cognitive-behavioral therapy: A clinician's guide.* Guilford Publications.

Torneke, N. (2010). *Learning RFT: An introduction to relational frame theory and its clinical application.* New Harbinger Publications.

Thrangu, K. (1993). *The practice of tranquility and insight: A guide to Tibetan Buddhist meditation.* Boston, MA: Shambhala Publications.

Trent, N. L., Park, C., Bercovitz, K., & Chapman, I. M. (2016). Trait socio-cognitive mindfulness is related to affective and cognitive empathy. *Journal of Adult Development, 23*(1), 62–67.

Tyler, P. (2018). *Christian mindfulness: Theology and practice.* SCM Press.

Unkelbach, C., Alves, H., & Koch, A. (2020). Negativity bias, positivity bias, and valence asymmetries: Explaining the differential processing of positive and negative information. *Advances in Experimental Social Psychology, 62,* 115–187.

Van Dam, N. T., van Vugt, M. K., Vago, D. R., Schmalzl, L., Saron, C. D., Olendzki, A., . . . & Meyer, D. E. (2018). Mind the hype: A critical evaluation and prescriptive agenda for research on mindfulness and meditation. *Perspectives on Psychological Science, 13*(1), 36–61.

Van Lysebeth, A. (1979). *Pranayama: The yoga of breathing.* Unwin Paperbacks.

VanElzakker, M. B., Dahlgren, M. K., Davis, F. C., Dubois, S., & Shin, L. M. (2014). From Pavlov to PTSD: The extinction of conditioned fear in rodents, humans, and anxiety disorders. *Neurobiology of Learning and Memory, 113,* 3–18. Doi: 10.1016/j.nlm.2013.11.014 PMID 24321650.

Veehof, M. M., Trompetter, H. R., Bohlmeijer, E. T., & Schreurs, K. M. G. (2016). Acceptance-and mindfulness-based interventions for the treatment of chronic pain: A meta-analytic review. *Cognitive Behaviour Therapy, 45*(1), 5–31.

Vestergaard-Poulsen, P., van Beek, M., Skewes, J., Bjarkam, C. R., Stubberup, M., Bertelsen, J., & Roepstorff, A. (2009). Long-term meditation is associated with increased gray matter density in the brain stem. *Neuroreport, 20*(2), 170–174.

Vidyanand, S. (2007). *Basic transformational yoga.* Sterling Publishers.

Von Zglinicki, T. (2002). Oxidative stress shortens telomeres. *Trends in Biochemical Sciences, 27*(7), 339–344.

Vonderlin, R., Biermann, M., Bohus, M., & Lyssenko, L. (2020). Mindfulness-based programs in the workplace: A meta-analysis of randomized controlled trials. *Mindfulness, 11*(7), 1579–1598.

Wallace, R. K. (1970). Physiological effects of transcendental meditation. *Science, 167*(3926), 1751–1754.

Walsh, M. M., & Arnold, K. A. (2020). The bright and dark sides of employee mindfulness: Leadership style and employee well-being. *Stress and Health, 36*(3), 287–298.

Walsh, R. A. (2008). Mindfulness and empathy. In S. F. Hick & T. Bien (Eds.), *Mindfulness and the therapeutic relationship* (pp. 72–86). Guilford Press.

Wang, D., Hagger, M. S., & Chatzisarantis, N. L. (2020). Ironic effects of thought suppression: A meta-analysis. *Perspectives on Psychological Science, 15*(3), 778–793.

Wason, P. C. (1960). On the failure to eliminate hypotheses in a conceptual task. *Quarterly Journal of Experimental Psychology, 12*, 129–140.

Watts, A. (1957). *The way of Zen.* New York: Pantheon.

Watts, A. (1958). *Nature, man and woman.* Pantheon Books.

Watts, A. (1965). *Swimming headless.* Retrieved from https://www.alanwatts.org/2-4-2-swimming-headless-part-2/

Watts, A. (1971). *Play and survival.* Retrieved from https://www.alanwatts.org/3-8-4-play-and-survival-part-4/

Watts, A. W. (2003). *Become what you are: Expanded edition.* Shambhala Publications.

Watts, A. (2004a). *Learning the human game [audio CD].* Louisville, CO: Sounds True.

Watts, A. (2004b). *Out of your mind: Essential listening from the Alan Watts Audio Archives* [audio CD]. Boulder, CO: Sounds True.

Watts, A. (2005). *Do you do it, or does it do you?.* Sounds True.

Watts, A. (2010). *Does it matter?: Essays on man's relation to materiality.* New World Library.

Watts, A. (2011). *Eastern wisdom, modern life: Collected talks: 1960–1969.* New World Library.

Watts, A. (2021). *Future of privacy and human organization.* Retrieved Jan 2, 2021, from https://www.organism.earth/library/document/future-of-privacy-and-human-organization

Wegner, D., Schneider, D., Carter, S., & White, T. (1987). Paradoxical effects of thought suppression. *Journal of Personality and Social Psychology, 53*, 5–13.

Wester, W. C., & Smith, A. H. (1984). *Clinical hypnosis: A multidisciplinary approach.* Lippincott Williams & Wilkins.

Wexler, J., & Ott, B. D. (2006). *The relationship between therapist mindfulness and the therapeutic alliance.* Doctoral dissertation, Massachusetts School of Professional Psychology.

Wiguna, R. I., Pamungkas, A. Y. F., Ningsih, H. E. W., & Hasan, M. I. (2018). Concept analysis of mindfulness based on Islam religion. *Jurnal Ilmu Keperawatan, 6*(2), 22–30.

Williams, M., Teasdale, J. D., Segal, Z. V., & Kabat-Zinn, J. (2007). *The mindful way through depression: Freeing yourself from chronic unhappiness.* Guilford Press.

Wimmer, L., Bellingrath, S., & von Stockhausen, L. (2020). Mindfulness training for improving attention regulation in university students: Is it effective? and do yoga and homework matter?. *Frontiers in Psychology, 11,* 719.

Wolpe, J. (1990). *The practice of behavior therapy.* Pergamon Press.

Wong, W. P., Camfield, D. A., Woods, W., Sarris, J., & Pipingas, A. (2015). Spectral power and functional connectivity changes during mindfulness meditation with eyes open: A magnetoencephalography (MEG) study in long-term meditators. *International Journal of Psychophysiology, 98*(1), 95–111.

Wonji Dharma. (2007a). *The barrier that has no gate (Wu Men Guan).* Buddha Dharma University Press.

Wonji Dharma. (2007b). *Buddhist precepts: A guide for western Buddhist Lay practitioners.* Buddha Dharma University Press.

Wonji Dharma. (2011). *Wu Shan Lu five mountain record.* Buddha Dharma University Press.

Wood, J. V., Elaine Perunovic, W. Q., & Lee, J. W. (2009). Positive self-statements: Power for some, peril for others. *Psychological Science, 20*(7), 860–866. Doi: 10.1111/j.1467-9280.2009.02370.x

Yalom, I. D. (1980). *Existential psychotherapy.* Basic Books.

Yapko, M. D. (2011). *Mindfulness and hypnosis: The power of suggestion to transform experience.* WW Norton & Company.

Yogananda, P. (1946). *Autobiography of a yogi.* Self-Realization Fellowship.

Yogi, M. M. (1963). *Science of being and art of living: Transcendental meditation.* Meridian.

Zuangzhi, Feng, G. F., & English, J. (2014). *Chuang Tsu: Inner chapters.* Hay House Publications.

Index

www.ingramcontent.com/pod-product-compliance
Lightning Source LLC
Chambersburg PA
CBHW070932030426
42336CB00014BA/2637